- UKULELE -

THE GREAT
AMERICAN SONGBOOK

THE COMPOSERS

MUSIC AND LYRICS FOR 100 STANDARDS FROM THE GOLDEN AGE OF AMERICAN SONG

T0079399

On the cover: Richard Rodgers & Oscar Hammerstein II (center) with (clockwise from upper left)
Cole Porter, Irving Berlin, Hoagy Carmichael, George Gershwin and Duke Ellington.

Photos of Ahlert, Arlen, Berlin, Burke, Van Heusen, Cahn, Coleman, Duke, Fain, Fields, Gershwin, Green,
Kahn, Koehler, Lane, Lerner & Loewe, Livingston & Evans, Loesser, McHugh, Mercer, Porter, Robin & Rainger,
Rodgers & Hart, Styne, Razaf, Warren, Washington, Whiting, and Young,
courtesy of Photofest.

Photos of Ellington, Strayhorn, and Waller,
courtesy of William "PoPsie" Randolph.
www.PoPsiePhotos.com

ISBN 978-1-5400-2103-8

Visit Hal Leonard Online at
www.halleonard.com

Contact us:
Hal Leonard
7777 West Bluemound Road
Milwaukee, WI 53213
Email: info@halleonard.com

In Europe, contact:
Hal Leonard Europe Limited
42 Wigmore Street
Marylebone, London, W1U 2RN
Email: info@halleonardeurope.com

In Australia, contact:
Hal Leonard Australia Pty. Ltd.
4 Lentara Court
Cheltenham, Victoria, 3192 Australia
Email: info@halleonard.com.au

CONTENTS

COMPOSER INDEX

THE COMPOSERS

FRED AHLERT
(1892-1953)

Born in New York City, Fred Ahlert combined perfect pitch and a law degree to build a song-writing career that included Broadway, Hollywood and the pop charts. He served as director of ASCAP (American Society of Composers, Authors and Publishers) for 19 years and as its president for one year. He created a number of hits with lyricist Joe Young, including "I'm Gonna Sit Right Down and Write Myself a Letter" (1935). With lyricist Roy Turk he created a string of hits that reappeared on the charts for many years, such as the 1928 "I'll Get By (As Long as I Have You)," which hit #3 in 1929 and #1 in 1944. "I Don't Know Why (I Just Do), hit #2 in 1931, and #16 in 1946.

HAROLD ARLEN
(1905-1986)

Harold Arlen, born Hyman Arluck, began his musical career singing in a Buffalo synagogue. He left school at 15 and began playing in a string of groups, eventually making his way to New York City. He once said of his songs, "No one would ever have known from those early songs that I would, could have, become a composer." Although he created numerous hits for the Cotton Club, Broadway, and films, he is best remembered for the songs he wrote for a certain 1939 MGM film that has never fallen from popularity: *The Wizard of Oz*. One of those songs was cut from the film and put back in three times before the film's release. That song, "Over the Rainbow," won him an Academy Award® in 1939.

IRVING BERLIN
(1888-1989)

Many of Berlin's more than 3000 songs, such as "God Bless America" and "White Christmas," remain a part of American popular culture today. Born Israel Isadore Baline in Russia, the songwriter came to the U.S. with his family in 1893. He left home at 15 to sing for pennies on the streets of New York. Writing both lyrics and music, Berlin captured universal emotions and sentiments in his music. Despite his scores of Broadway and film hits, Berlin never learned to put music on paper and could only play the piano in the key of F♯. He worked at a curious "transposing piano." The piano, which he called "the Buick" for the large lever used to ratchet the keyboard to new key areas, now resides at the Smithsonian. Berlin retired at age 86 and died peacefully in his sleep at 101.

JOHNNY BURKE
(1908-1964)

JIMMY VAN HEUSEN
(1913-1990)

Lyricist Johnny Burke and composer Jimmy Van Heusen were one of the most successful song-writing partnerships of the Tin Pan Alley era. The men were both well established by the time they began working together. Burke, who wrote words and music for such hits as "Pennies from Heaven," moved to Hollywood under contract with Paramount Pictures. At Paramount he worked on more than 50 films, including 25 films starring Bing Crosby. Van Heusen worked on more than 30 films, winning four Academy Awards for Best Song in a Motion Picture. Together Burke and Van Heusen formed the publishing company BurVan, Inc. After Burke retired from song writing in 1956, Van Heusen teamed up with lyricist Sammy Cahn and continued working as a music publisher.

SAMMY CAHN
(1913-1993)

Lyricist and librettist Sammy Cahn scored his first hit in 1937, with "Bei Mir Bist Du Schön," which put the Andrews Sisters on the pop music map. Writing with Jule Styne, Jimmy Van Heusen and others, Cahn wrote songs that were recorded by nearly every major singer of his time, with 89 of his songs recorded by Frank Sinatra. Cahn received more than 30 Oscar® nominations and won the award four times. Many of his songs remain a part of American popular culture, including "Love and Marriage," "Let It Snow, Let It Snow, Let It Snow" and "Three Coins in the Fountain." Written for the film *The Joker Is Wild*, "All the Way" won Cahn an Oscar®. Working with Van Heusen, he wrote "Come Fly with Me" in 1958, as the title song for an album by Frank Sinatra.

HOAGY CARMICHAEL
(1899-1981)

Born in Indiana to an itinerant farmer, Hoagland Howard Carmichael was practicing law in Florida when he decided to follow his star as a song writer. A few years earlier he had met and improvised for jazz cornetist Bix Beiderbecke, who asked him why he didn't write music. When Carmichael moved to New York in 1929, he looked up Beiderbecke, who introduced him to the hot young jazz players of the day. Carmichael's love and understanding of jazz coursed through his music and made his inventive tunes favorites of jazz musicians. In 1936 Carmichael moved to Hollywood, where he continued to write music and appear in films, on television and on radio. His "Stardust" (1927) has been hailed as the most often-recorded American song of all time.

CY COLEMAN
(1929-2004)

When a six-year-old Seymour Kaufman began giving piano recitals in New York, he was hailed as a child prodigy. As a young man he was a night club sensation, leading the Cy Coleman Trio. He turned to pop music, working for a time with Carolyn Leigh. Together they wrote a string of hits, including "The Best Is Yet to Come" and "Witchcraft." Coleman turned to Broadway and the hits kept coming, including "Big Spender" from the show *Sweet Charity*, written with Dorothy Fields. Between 1963 and 1997 he was nominated for 15 Tony® Awards, winning four, as well as three Emmy® Awards and two GRAMMY® Awards. One of his greatest strengths was the range of styles in which he was able to write, from country to jazz to R&B.

B.G. DeSylva
(1895-1950)
Lew Brown
(1893-1958)
Ray Henderson
(1896-1970)

Although lyricists B.G. "Buddy" DeSylva (left) and Lew Brown (right) and pianist and composer Ray Henderson (top) each scored hit songs working with various collaborators, together they made up the most famous songwriting/music publishing team of their era. The trio began contributing songs to Broadway shows in 1925, the same year they founded their own publishing company. In 1927, they created their own musical, *Good News*, which featured the song, "The Best Things in Life Are Free." The show ran for 557 performances on Broadway. In 1929 the trio sold their publishing company and relocated to Hollywood under a contract with Fox Studios. When DeSylva left the team in 1931, Brown and Henderson continued to produce hits. DeSylva became an executive producer at Paramount in 1941.

Walter Donaldson
(1893-1947)

Brooklyn-born Walter Donaldson left a Wall Street brokerage to take a shot at song writing. He scored his first hit in 1915 with "Back Home in Tennessee," followed by several more in the next few years. During World War I he entertained at Camp Upton in New York, where he met a young Irving Berlin. He joined Berlin's publishing company, Irving Berlin, Inc., after the war and continued to pen hits. In 1922 he began working with lyricist Gus Kahn. Together they wrote "Love Me or Leave Me" and "Makin' Whoopee!" for the 1928 musical *Nervous Wreck*. He also worked with other lyricists, including George Whiting, with whom he wrote "My Blue Heaven" in 1924. Donaldson moved to Hollywood as sound became a feature of films, writing for some of the earliest "talkies."

Vernon Duke
(1903-1969)

Born in Russia as Vladimir Dukelsky, Vernon Duke was of Lithuanian, Austrian and Spanish ancestry. He studied classical music in Kiev, becoming a close friend of composer Sergei Prokofiev. In 1920 his family fled revolution in Russia, arriving in the U.S. in 1921 via Constantinople (now Istanbul). In the U.S., Duke's classical composition caught the attention of George Gershwin, who encouraged the young composer to try his hand at popular music, and concocted a pen name for him. After a few years in Paris, Duke returned to the U.S. and created a reputation for writing sophisticated, urbane pop music. For many years he wrote classical music under his given name, and pop music as Vernon Duke. In the 1950s he began to use the name Duke for all of his work.

Duke Ellington
(1899-1974)

Often hailed as the most important musician of the 20th century, Edward Kennedy "Duke" Ellington was the grandson of a former slave. Born in Washington, D.C., Ellington arrived in New York City in 1923 and began leading his own band a year later. Ellington wrote some 2,000 pieces, including songs, musical comedies, film scores and suites. He played the White House and toured Europe, received the French Legion of Honor and the American Presidential Medal of Freedom, and was awarded honorary doctorates by Yale and Harvard. He was reported to have played more than 20,000 performances by the end of his long career. After World War II, when big band music took a back seat to rock 'n' roll, Ellington used his royalties to pay his band members' salaries.

SAMMY FAIN
(1902-1989)

Born Samuel Feinberg in New York City and raised upstate, Sammy Fain returned to New York as a music publisher's stock boy after high school. But the self-taught musician wanted to write songs. His dream came true when he met lyricist Irving Kahal in the 1920s. The pair worked together until 1942. They moved to Hollywood in 1930 to write songs for films, but they continued to write for Broadway. The pair wrote "I Can Dream, Can't I?" and "I'll Be Seeing You" in 1938 for the show *Right This Way*, which flopped. After Kahal's death, Fain worked with a number of lyricists, including Paul Francis Webster. Fain, who contributed songs to more than 30 motion pictures, was nominated for nine Oscars®, winning twice.

DOROTHY FIELDS
(1905-1974)

Dorothy Fields' lyric-writing career spanned five decades. She dreamed of becoming an actress, but her father Lew Fields, one of the most powerful theater producers of his time, wouldn't allow it. Instead, she began writing lyrics, scoring her first hit in 1928 with "I Can't Give You Anything but Love." Over the years she worked with many songwriters, including Jerome Kern. Together they wrote "A Fine Romance" in 1936. She and Kern won an Academy Award in 1936 for "The Way You Look Tonight." In the 1940s Fields branched out to writing books for musicals and had a number of successes on Broadway. She worked with Cy Coleman in the 1950s and '60s, writing "Big Spender" and other songs for *Sweet Charity*. Fields was known for her touching lyrics.

GEORGE GERSHWIN
(1898-1937)

The son of Russian immigrants, Jacob Gershvin was born in Brooklyn and raised on the Lower East Side of Manhattan. He dropped out of school to try his hand at music and was working as a Tin Pan Alley song plugger by age 16. At 19 his song "Swanee" became a million-selling hit, thanks in part to Al Jolson's rendition of it in the show *Sinbad*. That year Gershwin wrote his first complete Broadway score, *La, La Lucille*. He soon began working with his lyricist brother Ira, creating a long string of hit shows and songs. Gershwin wrote 28 shows and one opera, contributed songs to 19 others shows and seven films, and composed several orchestral works. He died during surgery for a brain tumor at age 38.

JOHNNY GREEN
(1908-1989)

Born in 1908 in New York City, Johnny Green wrote jazz standards, conducted classical orchestras around the world, conducted an orchestra for Jack Benny, and wrote music for Broadway, film and television. Accepted at Harvard at age 15, Green served as music director at MGM for ten years. He also served as chairman of the Academy of Motion Picture Arts and Sciences. He won five Academy Awards® for scores to such films as *Easter Parade*, *An American in Paris*, *West Side Story* and *Oliver!*. Green dedicated "Out of Nowhere" to the first of his three wives. "Body and Soul" has become something of a rite-of-passage piece for saxophonists, thanks to exceptional recordings of the piece by Coleman Hawkins (1939) and John Coltrane (1960).

GUS KAHN
(1886-1941)

One of the most productive of the Tin Pan Alley lyricists, Gus Kahn was born in Germany and raised in Chicago. He worked as a song plugger for a time in Chicago before finding success as a lyricist. Kahn worked with composer and bandleader Isham Jones and later with Al Jolson. Several of Kahn's songs were heard in Jolson's 1927 film, *The Jazz Singer*. He worked on Broadway and in films at the same time, scoring three Academy Award® nominations and winning the Best Score Award in 1934 for *One Night of Love*. Collaborating with a virtual who's who of the music industry, his songs have appeared in more than 200 films.

JEROME KERN
(1885-1945)

Born in New York City, Jerome Kern completed 100 show scores, more than 650 songs and essentially redefined musical theater. Kern's career began in London, where his songs began to appear on the stage. He then began interpolating songs into European operettas adapted for the American stage. After 1915, his original musicals began appearing in New York. Working with Guy Bolton and P.G. Wodehouse, Kern created musical theater productions that integrated plot and songs and had an anchor in reality. In 1927 he and Oscar Hammerstein II created what would prove to be Kern's most important work, *Show Boat*. With songs integral to the show's plot, *Show Boat* redirected Broadway composers to writing music that advanced plot or characters within a show, rather than tunes that could be interpolated into any number of shows.

TED KOEHLER
(1894-1973)

From an early career in the photography industry to a gig playing piano for silent films and then producing nightclub acts, Washington, D.C.-born lyricist Ted Koehler spent three decades writing timeless songs. He wrote for Broadway in the 1920s, moving to Hollywood in the 1930s. His film credits include *Springtime in the Rockies*, *Hollywood Canteen*, *Summer Stock* and three Academy Award® nominations. He collaborated with some of the great songwriters of the day, including Harold Arlen, with whom he wrote "Stormy Weather," "I've Got the World on a String," and "Let's Fall in Love." He also collaborated with Duke Ellington, Ray Henderson, Burton Lane, Jimmy McHugh and Harry Warren.

BURTON LANE
(1912-1992)

One of Burton Lane's most enduring achievements was his discovery of an 11-year-old performer named Francis Gumm, who would become known to the world as Judy Garland. The New Yorker signed his first contract, with Remick Music, at age 15, launching a career that would flourish equally on Broadway and in Hollywood. He wrote for more than 30 films and was twice nominated for Academy Awards®, including for "Too Late Now" in 1951. He collaborated with some of the era's greats, including E.Y. Harburg, writing *Finian's Rainbow* and the hit "How Are Things in Glocca Morra," and Alan Jay Lerner, writing *On a Clear Day You Can See Forever*. Lane served ten terms as president of the American Guild of Authors and Composers.

ALAN JAY LERNER
(1918-1986)
FREDERICK LOEWE
(1901-1988)

Lerner and Loewe were the dominant names of Broadway for more than a decade, scoring huge successes with shows like *Camelot*, *Brigadoon* and *My Fair Lady*. The Harvard- and Juilliard-educated Lerner and the older, Austrian-born Loewe met and began working together in 1942. In 1947 they opened *Brigadoon*. With *My Fair Lady*, which ran for nine years, they created one of the most successful shows in the history of American theater, breaking all existing records of the time. The 1964 film won seven Academy Awards®. The pair also created the 1958 film *Gigi*, which won nine Oscars®. Lerner worked independently on projects as well, including *An American in Paris*, which won him an Academy Award® in 1951.

JAY LIVINGSTON
(1915-2001)
RAY EVANS
(1915-2007)

The work of Jay Livingston and Ray Evans is ubiquitous. Their songs, like "Mona Lisa" (1949) and "Que Sera, Sera" (1935), both of which won Academy Awards®, and the Christmas standard "Silver Bells," have taken on lives of their own. In the world of television, they created the theme songs for shows like "Bonanza" and "Mr. Ed." The two succeeded in every genre they entered. They wrote for Broadway shows and for nightclub acts, including providing all of the material for Bob Hope's personal appearances for many years. Called "the last great songwriters of Hollywood," the duo was honored by the Academy of Motion Picture Arts and Sciences in 1996 with an evening dedicated to their work.

FRANK LOESSER
(1910-1969)

Composer and lyricist Frank Loesser was born into a musical family in New York City. He drifted from job to job for a time before trying his hand at song writing. Although his 1930 try at Broadway was not a success, it led to a 1936 contract with Universal Pictures. He worked with several composers until 1942, when he wrote the music and lyrics to "Praise the Lord and Pass the Ammunition." The hit song set him on the path of writing both music and lyrics and led to successes like *Guys and Dolls* (1950) on Broadway and *Hans Christian Andersen* (1952) on film. His music appeared in nearly 90 films and 13 Broadway shows, not including revues and revivals. He received several Tony® Awards, an Academy Award® and a Pulitzer Prize.

JIMMY McHUGH
(1893-1969)

Boston-born Jimmy McHugh went from accompanying opera rehearsals to writing for the Cotton Club in the early 1920s. He began working with lyricist Dorothy Fields in the late 1920s, with whom he created such gems as "On the Sunny Side of the Street" (1930) and "Don't Blame Me" (1932). The duo moved to Hollywood and began writing for films. McHugh also collaborated for many years with Harold Adamson, with whom he won a Presidential Certificate of Merit during World War II. His other collaborators included Johnny Mercer, Frank Loesser, Jerome Kern and Gus Kahn. McHugh was nominated for five Academy Awards®. He served as the director of ASCAP (American Society of Composers, Authors and Publishers) throughout the 1960s.

JOHNNY MERCER
(1909-1976)

Born into old money in Savannah, Johnny Mercer headed for New York and an acting career when his family fortune vaporized. He began writing songs and started singing with the Paul Whiteman Band. His genius for lyric writing sent him to Hollywood in 1933, where he wrote songs for films and sang with the likes of Bing Crosby and Benny Goodman's band. Mercer and songwriter Buddy DeSylva founded the legendary Capitol Records, with Mercer as president. Mercer was nominated for 19 Academy Awards® and received four, including a 1961 Best Song Oscar® for "Moon River" (*Breakfast at Tiffany's*, with Henry Mancini). Mercer, who generated hits for more than 40 years, founded the Songwriter's Hall of Fame.

COLE PORTER
(1891-1964)

The king of wit and sophistication, Cole Porter was born to wealth in Indiana. He was educated at Yale, where his witty songs made him the toast of the campus. He entered Harvard in law, but soon switched to music, moving to New York in 1916 and then Paris. He had a long marriage, although one of deep friendship rather than romance, and lived an international life of opulence, finally finding musical success in the late 1920s. Falling from a horse in 1937, Porter lost the use of his legs and began a twenty-year period of constant pain. Yet he continued to write, creating such masterpieces as *Kiss Me, Kate* (1948) and *Can-Can* (1953). The deaths of his mother and wife in the 1950s combined with his deteriorating health left him depressed and reclusive in his last years.

LEO ROBIN
(1900-1984)
RALPH RAINGER
(1900-1942)

Leo Robin and Ralph Rainger were one of the great songwriting teams of the 1930s. Robin, who had aspirations as a playwright, began writing songs for Broadway with various collaborators during the 1920s. He and Rainger, who abandoned law for music, had a 1930 hit with "I'll Take an Option on You." They moved to Hollywood under contract with Paramount and wrote for a string of hit movies, eventually moving to Twentieth Century Fox in 1939. They received the Academy Award® for Best Song in 1938 for "Thanks for the Memory," which appeared in *Big Broadcast of 1938*. After Rainger's death in a plane crash in 1942, Robin wrote with a number of collaborators, including Jule Styne, creating "Diamonds Are a Girl's Best Friend" for *Gentlemen Prefer Blondes* in 1949.

RICHARD RODGERS
(1902-1979)
OSCAR HAMMERSTEIN II
(1895-1960)

The story of musical theater in America cannot be told without a lengthy chapter devoted to Richard Rodgers. For more than six decades his music was the gold standard in theater, and later in films. His work and influence reached beyond these shores and had an impact on British theater as well. The second of his two principal collaborators, Oscar Hammerstein II, is remembered as the man who had the greatest impact on taking American musical theater from diversion to a meaningful art form. He first created shock waves with the book and lyrics for the groundbreaking *Show Boat*, with Jerome Kern. Together, Rodgers and Hammerstein wrote nine musicals that further changed the musical theater landscape, beginning with their innovative musical play, *Oklahoma!* (1943). They were unafraid of sensitive issues, such as the topic of racism in *South Pacific* (1949). Other shows include *Carousel*, *The King and I* and *The Sound of Music*.

RICHARD RODGERS
(1902-1979)
LORENZ HART
(1895-1943)

Richard Rodgers began his musical career in remarkably fruitful collaboration with lyricist Lorenz Hart, whom he met at Columbia University. The pair produced two shows each season during the 1920s, moving to Hollywood for the first half of the 1930s to write for a dozen films. They returned to Broadway in 1936 for some of their finest work, beginning with *On Your Toes* (1936) and *Babes in Arms* (1937). The pair created unforgettable songs built of mesmerizing music and clever, often monosyllabic rhymes. Beneath his keen mind and quick wit, Hart battled both personal demons and alcoholism, the latter of which killed him at age 48. Hart's heartaches often found voice in touching lyrics, like those to "My Funny Valentine," written for *Babes in Arms*.

BILLY STRAYHORN
(1915-1967)

Perhaps no one other than Duke Ellington had as big an impact on the Ellington band than Dayton-born composer Billy "Sweet Pea" Strayhorn. In the 25 years he collaborated with Ellington, he wrote much of the music that defined the band's sound and style, including its theme song, "Take the "A" Train." Strayhorn's talent was evident in his teens. He received a fairly extensive classical training, which allowed him to coach Lena Horne in classical music. He also arranged, in collaboration with Ellington, pieces like Tchaikovsky's *Nutcracker Suite* and Grieg's *Peer Gynt Suite*. After Strayhorn's death, Ellington recorded what is deemed one of his greatest albums, *And His Mother Called Him Bill*, in tribute.

JULE STYNE
(1905-1994)

London-born Jule Styne came to Chicago as a child, with his family. Although Styne performed with the Detroit and Chicago Symphonies as a youngster, he turned to popular music as an adult, playing and arranging with jazz bands and forming a band of his own in the 1930s. He eventually moved to Hollywood to write and arrange music for films, and also worked as a vocal coach. He worked with several lyricists during his career, including Frank Loesser and Leo Robin. Styne met lyricist Sammy Cahn in 1942, and together the two began turning out hits for films and Broadway, including the Oscar®-winning, "Three Coins in the Fountain." He was nominated for nine other Oscars® and won a Tony®, an Emmy® and two GRAMMY Awards.

THOMAS "FATS" WALLER
(1904-1943)

ANDY RAZAF
(1895-1973)

A preacher's kid from New York City, Fats Waller learned to play the organ at his father's church. He began singing and playing in clubs, eventually forming and leading his own band and touring the world. Famous for such quips as "One never knows, do one?", Waller died in Kansas City, on a train from Los Angeles to New York. He was 39. Although Waller collaborated with several lyricists, he worked most often with Andy Razaf. Born Andriamanantena Paul Razafinkarefo in Washington, D.C. to a Madagascar nobleman, Razaf is remembered as the most prolific African-American lyric writer of his era. Together, Waller and Razaf turned out a spate of remarkable hits. Razaf turned to newspaper writing in the 1950s, a career he maintained for the rest of his life.

NED WASHINGTON
(1901-1976)

VICTOR YOUNG
(1900-1956)

HARRY WARREN
(1893-1981)

The composer of such familiar hits as "Jeepers Creepers" (with Johnny Mercer) and "Shuffle Off to Buffalo" (with Al Dubin), composer Harry Warren was born Salvatore Guaragna in Brooklyn. He struck out on his own at age 15, working with touring carnivals and doing backstage work for a vaudeville theater. During World War I, Warren served in the U.S. Navy, trying his hand at song writing after the war. In 1933 he headed for Hollywood to work on the film *42nd Street* with Dubin. He and Dubin would write about 20 musicals together. In 1942, Warren's song "Chattanooga Choo Choo" won Glenn Miller the first gold record ever presented. Warren also wrote a number of scores for dramatic films, including *An Affair to Remember* (1957). He was nominated for 11 Oscars® and won three.

Lyricist Ned Washington entered the world of show business as a vaudeville emcee and talent agent. He began writing lyrics in collaboration with Tin Pan Alley songwriters, moving to Hollywood in 1934 with an MGM contract in hand. He would eventually write for Republic, Paramount, Warner Bros. and Disney. His principal collaborator was composer Victor Young, but Washington also worked with many of the era's great songwriters. Washington was nominated for 11 Academy Awards®, winning Best Original Music twice, including the 1940 Oscar® for "When You Wish Upon a Star," from the film *Pinocchio*. Among his enduring songs, "The Nearness of You" (1940, with Hoagy Carmichael) was popularized by the Glenn Miller Orchestra in the 1940s and reappeared as recently as 2004, in the film *Twisted*.

RICHARD WHITING
(1891-1938)

Born in Peoria, Illinois and educated at the Harvard Military School in Los Angeles, Richard Whiting was a largely self-taught musician. Among his many Tin Pan Alley hits was the World War I ballad, "'Til We Meet Again." From 1917 to about 1927, Whiting worked in New York and wrote scores for Broadway shows. He began writing for films in 1929 with Maurice Chevalier's American film debut, *Innocents of Paris*. "My Ideal," composed with Newell Chase with lyrics by Leo Robin, was written for Chevalier to sing in the film *Playboy of Paris*. Whiting's film work also included "On the Good Ship Lollipop," for Shirley Temple in the 1934 film *Bright Eyes*. Whiting's daughter, Margaret Whiting, became one of the country's favorite pop singers following her father's 1938 death.

From the concert stage to Hollywood, Victor Young took an unlikely path to writing music for films. Born in Chicago, he moved to Poland as a child to study the violin. He toured Europe as a concert violinist before returning to the U.S. and entering the world of pop music as a violinist and arranger. He also worked in radio programming in Chicago and New York. Young moved to Hollywood in the mid 1930s where he became one of the country's most prolific composers of film music, composing scores to more than 350 films. He received 22 Academy Award® nominations, receiving four in one year on two separate occasions. He was awarded only one Oscar®, for the score to *Around the World in Eighty Days* (1956). The award came shortly after his death.

This page is intentionally left blank
to avoid unnecessary page turns.

Ac-cent-tchu-ate the Positive

from the Motion Picture HERE COME THE WAVES
Lyric by Johnny Mercer
Music by Harold Arlen

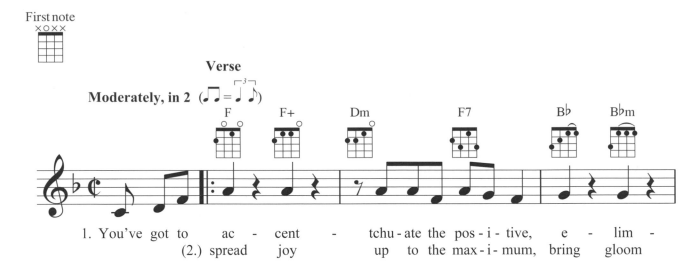

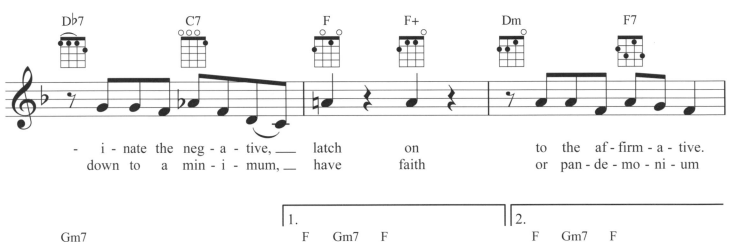

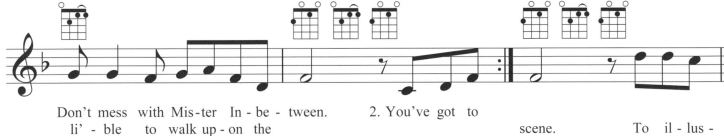

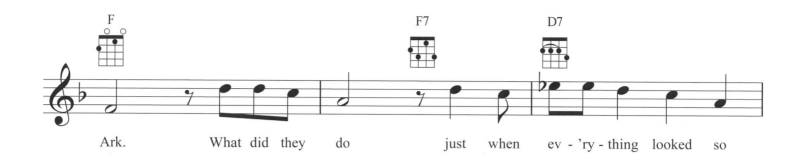

Ark.   What did they   do   just when   ev - ’ry - thing looked so

Outro-Verse

dark?   "Man," they said, "We bet - ter   ac - cent -

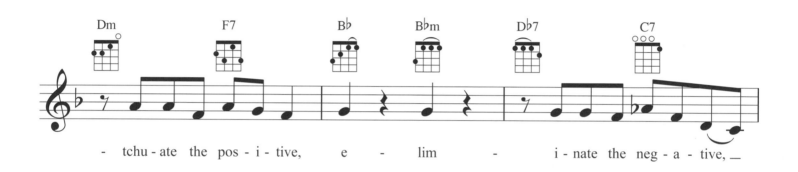

- tchu - ate the pos - i - tive,   e - lim   -   i - nate the neg - a - tive, __

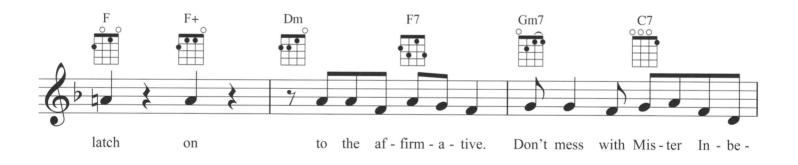

latch   on   to the af - firm - a - tive.   Don't mess with Mis - ter In - be -

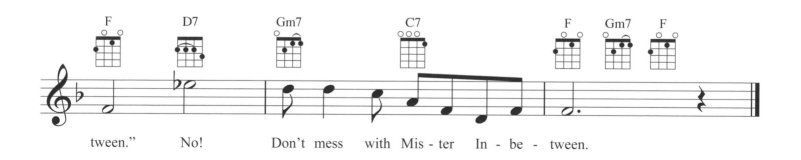

tween."   No!   Don't mess with Mis - ter In - be - tween.

Ain't Misbehavin'

from AIN'T MISBEHAVIN'
Words by Andy Razaf
Music by Thomas "Fats" Waller and Harry Brooks

All the Things You Are

from VERY WARM FOR MAY
Lyrics by Oscar Hammerstein II
Music by Jerome Kern

All the Way

from THE JOKER IS WILD
Words by Sammy Cahn
Music by James Van Heusen

1. When some-bod-y loves you, it's no good un-less he loves you
2. When some-bod-y needs you, it's no good un-less she needs you

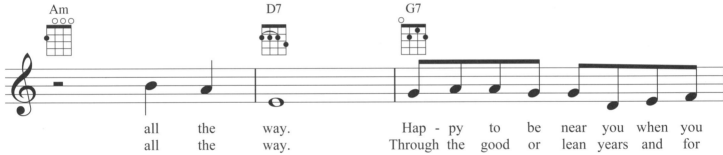

all   the   way.   Hap-py to be near you when you
all   the   way.   Through the good or lean years and for

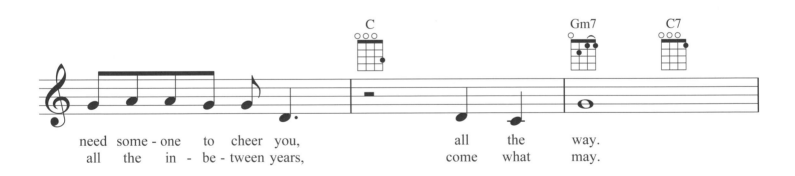

need some-one to cheer you,   all   the   way.
all   the in-be-tween years,   come what may.

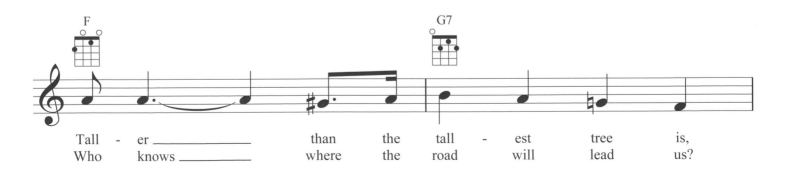

Tall-er _____   than the tall-est tree is,
Who knows _____   where the road will lead us?

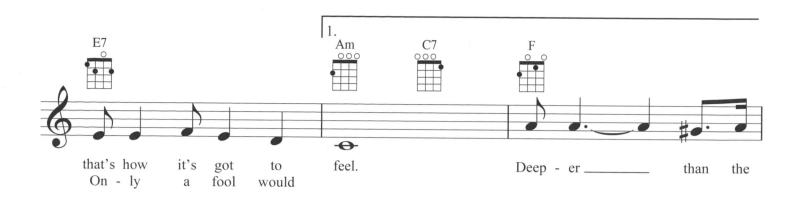

E7   1.   Am   C7   F

that's how   it's   got   to   feel.   Deep - er _____ than the
On - ly   a   fool   would

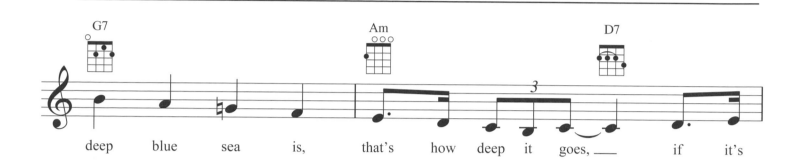

G7   Am   D7

deep   blue   sea   is,   that's   how   deep   it   goes, ____   if   it's

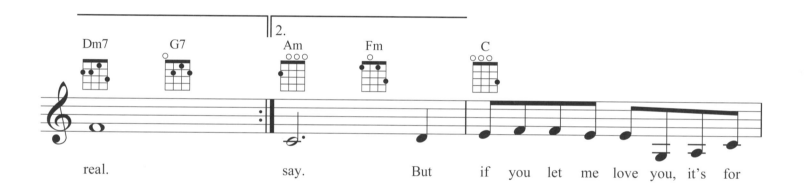

Dm7   G7   2.   Am   Fm   C

real.   say.   But   if   you   let   me   love   you,   it's   for

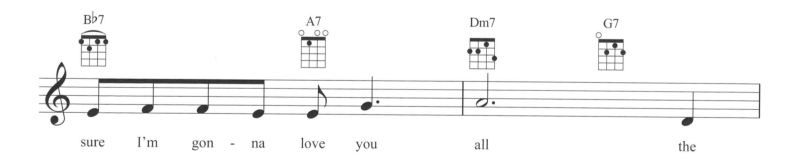

B♭7   A7   Dm7   G7

sure   I'm   gon - na   love   you   all   the

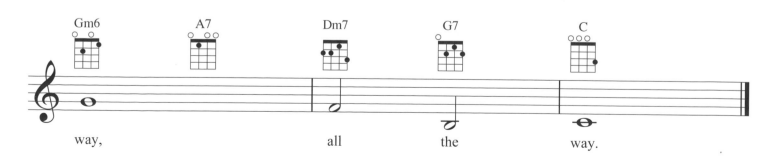

Gm6   A7   Dm7   G7   C

way,   all   the   way.

April in Paris

Words by E.Y. "Yip" Harburg
Music by Vernon Duke

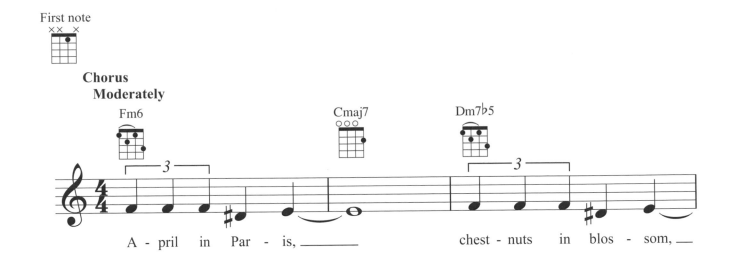

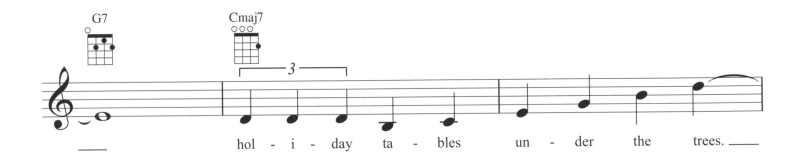

A - pril in Par - is, _____ chest - nuts in blos - som, __

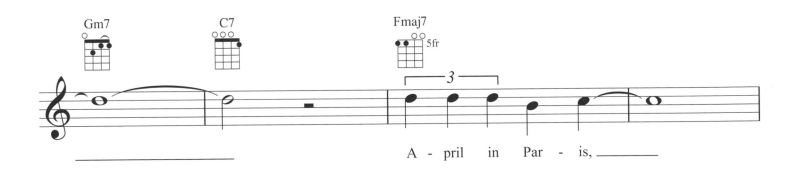

_____ hol - i - day ta - bles un - der the trees. ___

A - pril in Par - is, _____

this is a feel - ing _____ no one can ev - er _____ re -

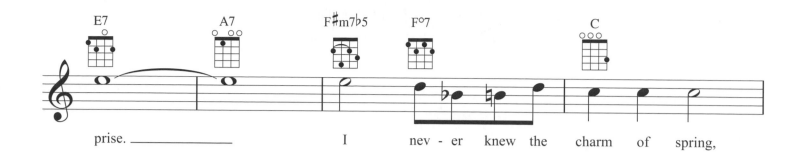

prise. _____ I nev - er knew the charm of spring,

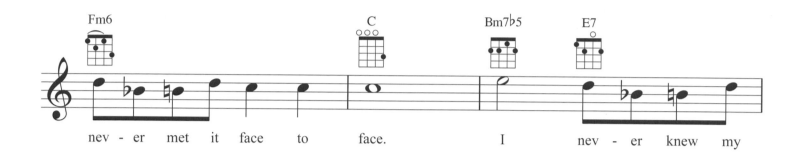

nev - er met it face to face. I nev - er knew my

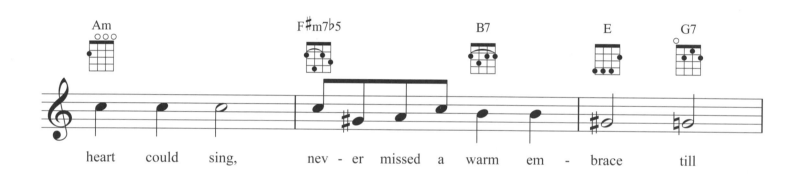

heart could sing, nev - er missed a warm em - brace till

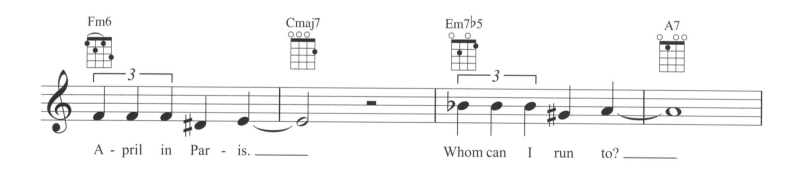

A - pril in Par - is. _____ Whom can I run to? _____

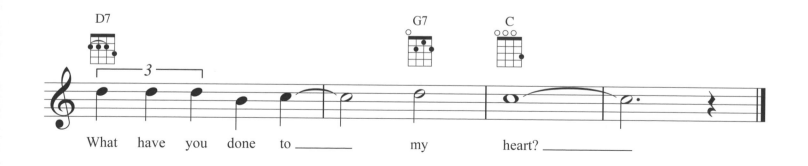

What have you done to _____ my heart? _____

Autumn in New York

Words and Music by Vernon Duke

The Best Is Yet to Come

Music by Cy Coleman
Lyrics by Carolyn Leigh

First note

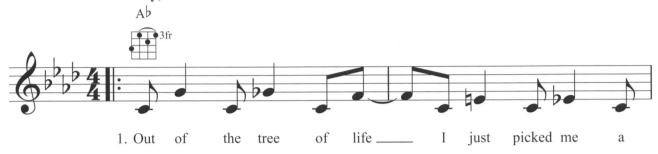

fine? _____ You think you've seen the sun _

_____ but you ain't seen it shine. _____ Wait till the warm-up's

un - der - way, ___ wait till our lips have met, ___

wait till you see that sun - shine day, ___ you ain't seen noth - in' yet! _

Chorus

_ The best is yet to come ___ and, babe, won't it be

fine? _____ The best is yet to come, _

ground. _____ Wait till you're locked in

my em - brace, _ wait till I draw you near. ____

Wait till you see that sun - shine place, ain't noth - in' like it here! _

Outro-Chorus

____ The best is yet to come ___ and, babe, won't it be

fine? _____ The best is yet to come, _

____ come _ the day _ you're mine. _____

The Best Things in Life Are Free

from GOOD NEWS!
Music and Lyrics by B.G. DeSylva, Lew Brown and Ray Henderson

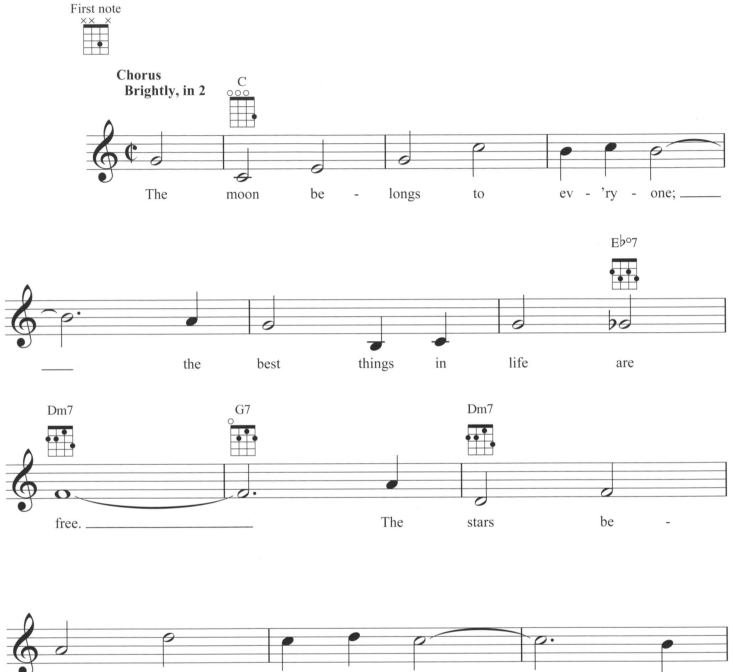

The moon be - longs to ev - 'ry - one; ____ the best things in life are free. ____ The stars be - long to ev - 'ry - one; ____ they gleam there for you and me. ____

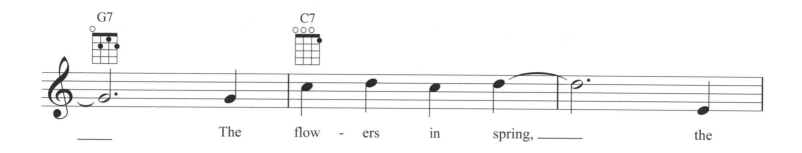

The flow - ers in spring, _____ the

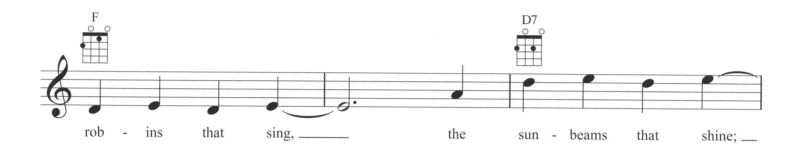

rob - ins that sing, _____ the sun - beams that shine; __

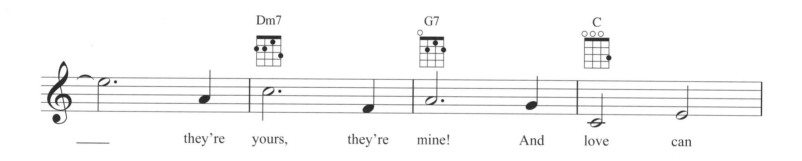

_____ they're yours, they're mine! And love can

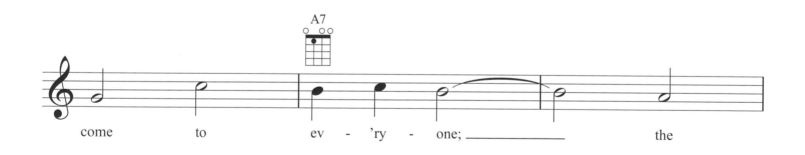

come to ev - 'ry - one; _____ the

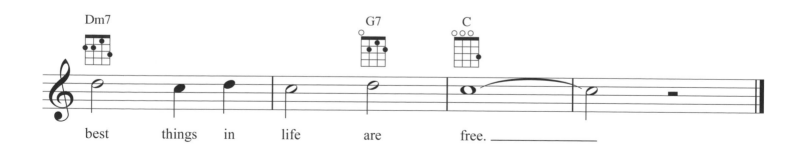

best things in life are free. _____

Beyond the Blue Horizon

from the Paramount Picture MONTE CARLO
Words by Leo Robin
Music by Richard A. Whiting and W. Franke Harling

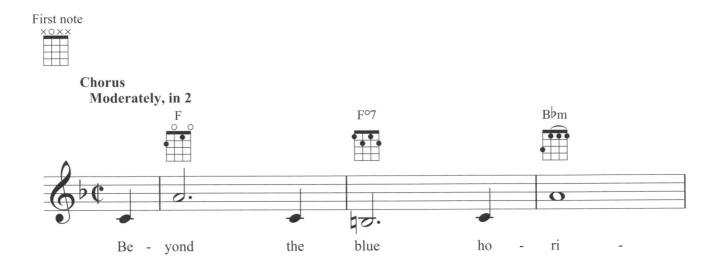

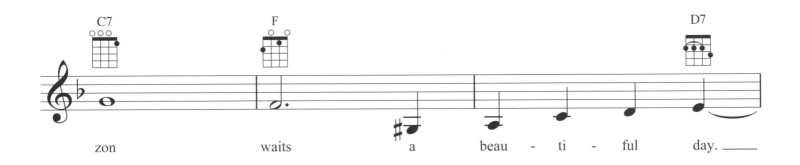

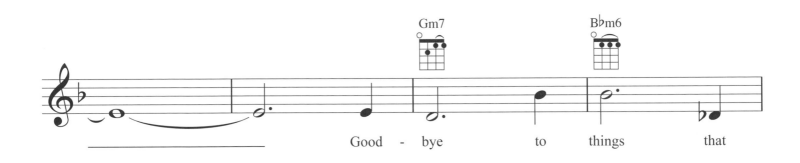

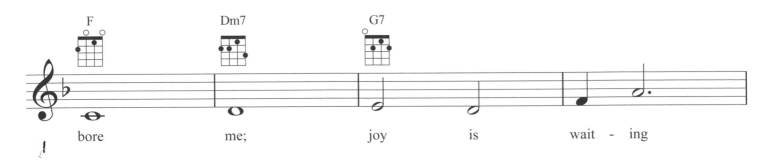

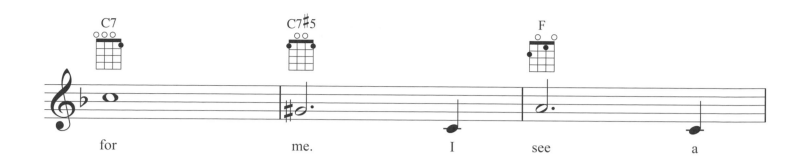

for   me.   I see   a

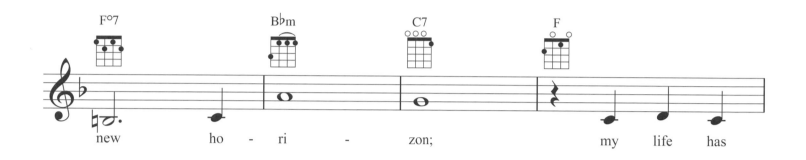

new   ho - ri - zon;   my   life   has

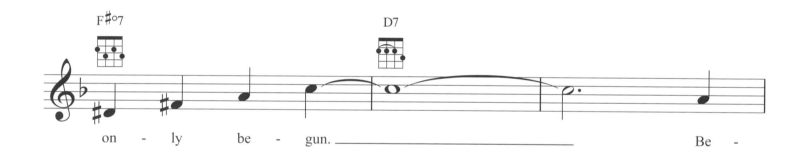

on - ly be - gun. _____   Be -

yond   the   blue   ho - ri - zon   lies   a

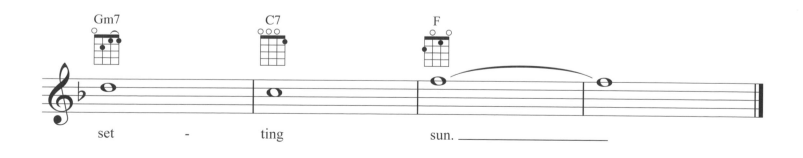

set - ting   sun. _____

Blue Skies

from BETSY
Words and Music by Irving Berlin

Big Spender

from SWEET CHARITY
Music by Cy Coleman
Lyrics by Dorothy Fields

First note

Moderately, with a beat

§ Chorus

The min-ute you walked in the joint, I could see you were a

man of dis-tinc-tion, a real big spend-er! Good look-ing,

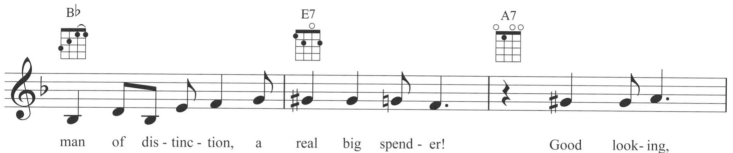

so re-fined. ___ Say, would-n't you like to know what's go-ing

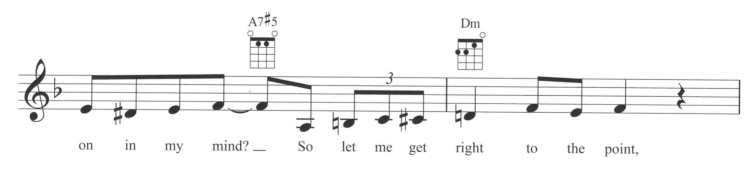

on in my mind? ___ So let me get right to the point,

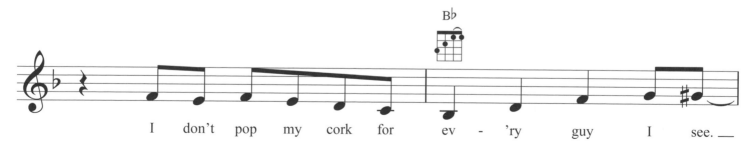

I don't pop my cork for ev-'ry guy I see. ___

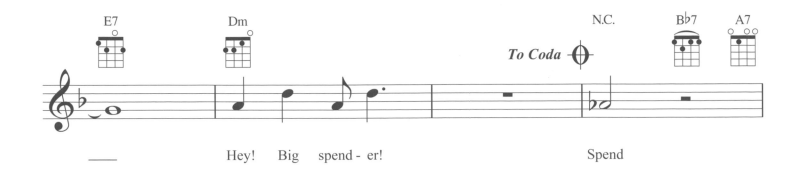

Hey! Big spend-er! Spend

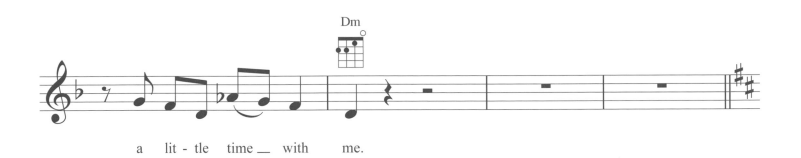

a lit-tle time __ with me.

Bridge

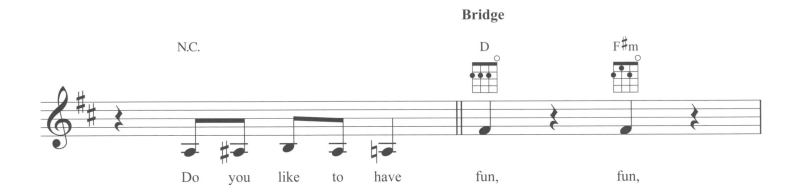

Do you like to have fun, fun,

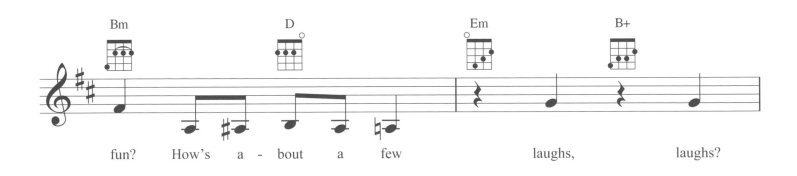

fun? How's a-bout a few laughs, laughs?

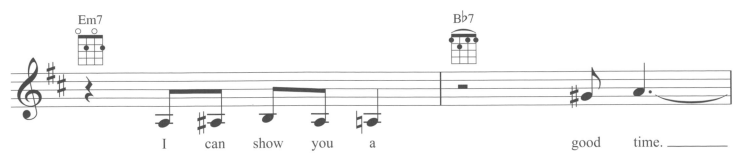

I can show you a good time. _____

Let me show you a good time. _____ The min-ute you

Coda

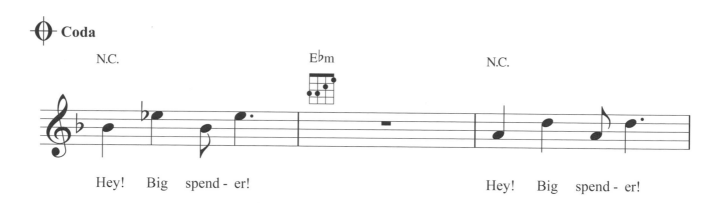

Hey! Big spend - er! Hey! Big spend - er!

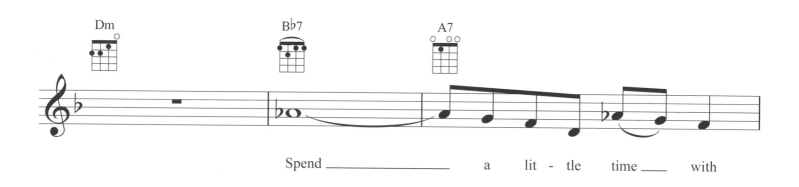

Spend _____ a lit - tle time ___ with

Outro

me. Spend a lit - tle time ___ with me.

Spend a lit - tle time ___ with me. _____

Body and Soul

from THREE'S A CROWD
Words by Edward Heyman, Robert Sour and Frank Eyton
Music by John Green

you'd turn a - way ro - mance.

Are you pre - tend - ing? It looks like the end - ing un -

less I could have one more chance to prove, dear.

Outro-Verse

My life a wreck you're mak - ing, you know I'm yours for

just the tak - ing; I'd glad - ly sur - ren - der

my - self to you, bod - y and soul!

Button Up Your Overcoat

from FOLLOW THRU

Words and Music by B.G. DeSylva, Lew Brown and Ray Henderson

Bridge

long   to   me!   Be care - ful   cross - ing streets,
long   to   me!   Don't sit on   hor - nets'   tails,

oo - oo!   Don't eat meats,   oo - oo!   Cut out sweets,
oo - oo,   or on nails,   oo - oo,   or third rails,

oo - oo!   You'll get   a pain and ru -   in your tum - tum!
oo - oo!   You'll get   a pain and ru -   in your tum - tum!

Outro-Verse

Keep a - way from boot - leg hootch ___   when you're on   a
Don't go out with col - lege boys ___   when you're on   a

spree.   Take   good ___   care of your - self; ___   you be -
spree.   Take   good ___   care of your - self; ___   you be -

long   to   me.
long   to me.

Buttons and Bows

from the Paramount Picture THE PALEFACE
Words and Music by Jay Livingston and Ray Evans

2. **Bridge**

F7   B♭

_____ I'll love you in buck - skin or

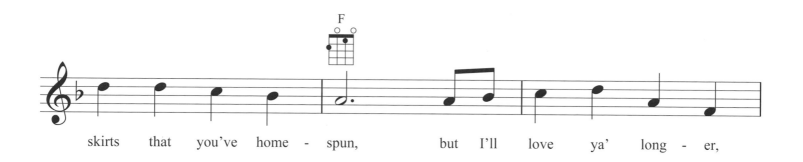

F

skirts that you've home - spun, but I'll love ya' long - er,

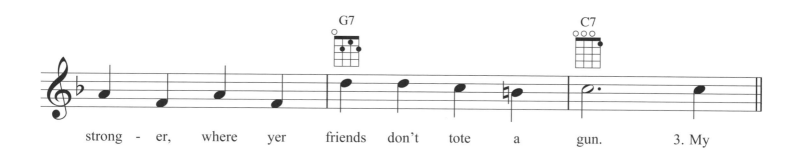

G7   C7

strong - er, where yer friends don't tote a gun. 3. My

Verse

F   Dm   F   Dm   F   Dm

bones de - nounce the buck - board bounce, and the cac - tus hurts my

F   Dm   B♭   F   B♭

toes. Let's va - moose where gals keep us - in' those

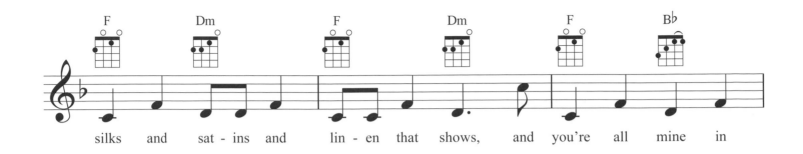

silks and sat - ins and lin - en that shows, and you're all mine in

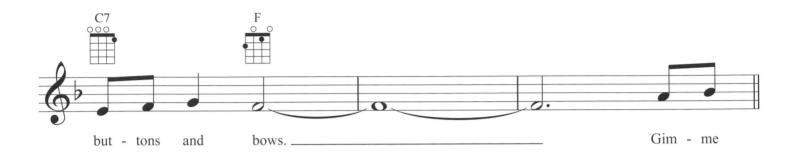

but - tons and bows. _____ Gim - me

Outro

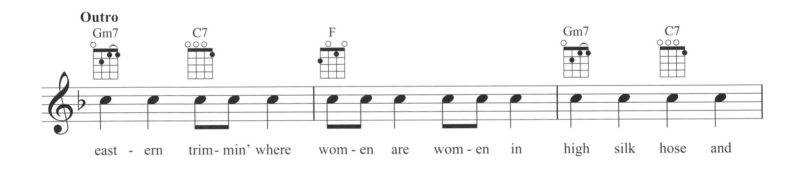

east - ern trim - min' where wom - en are wom - en in high silk hose and

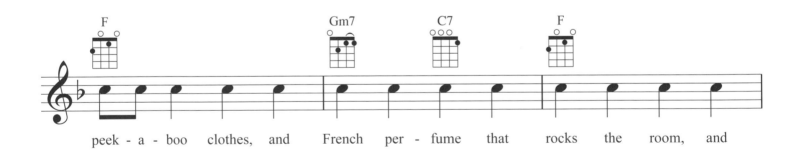

peek - a - boo clothes, and French per - fume that rocks the room, and

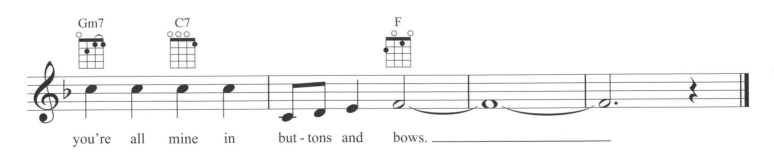

you're all mine in but - tons and bows. _____

Cheek to Cheek

from the RKO Radio Motion Picture TOP HAT
Words and Music by Irving Berlin

First note

Chorus
Moderately, in 2

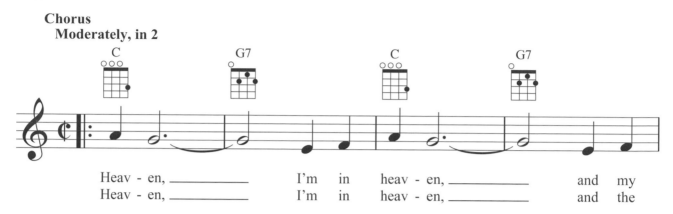

Heav - en, _____ I'm in heav - en, _____ and my
Heav - en, _____ I'm in heav - en, _____ and the

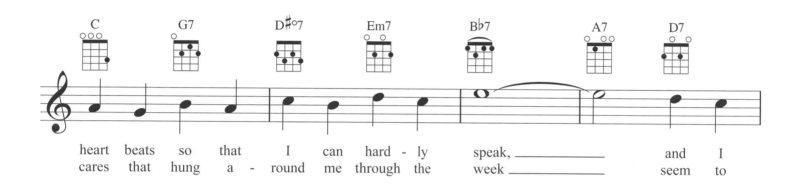

heart beats so that I can hard - ly speak, _____ and I
cares that hung a - round me through the week _____ seem to

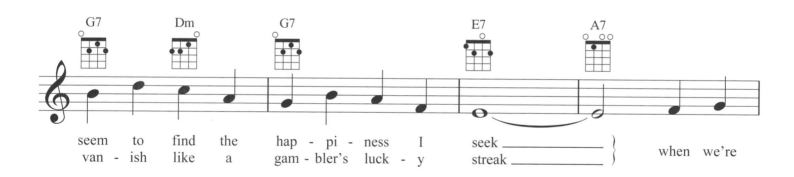

seem to find the hap - pi - ness I seek _____ } when we're
van - ish like a gam - bler's luck - y streak _____ }

1.

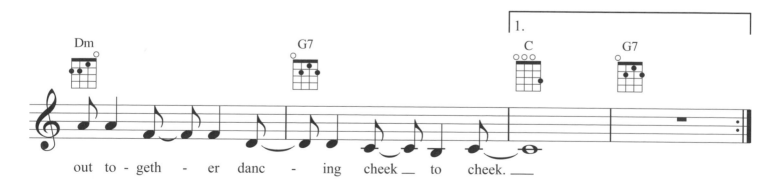

out to - geth - er danc - ing cheek ___ to cheek. ___

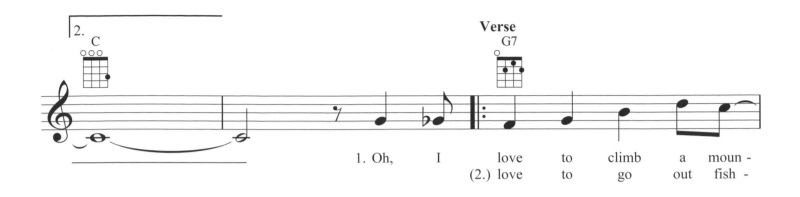

Verse

1. Oh, I love to climb a moun-
(2.) love to go out fish-

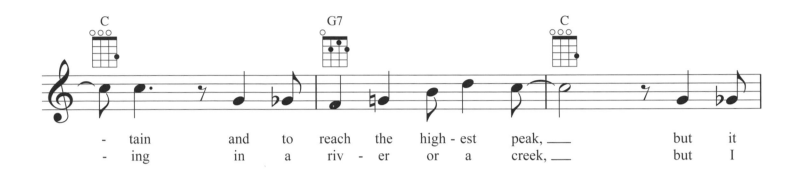

- tain and to reach the high - est peak, ___ but it
- ing in a riv - er or a creek, ___ but I

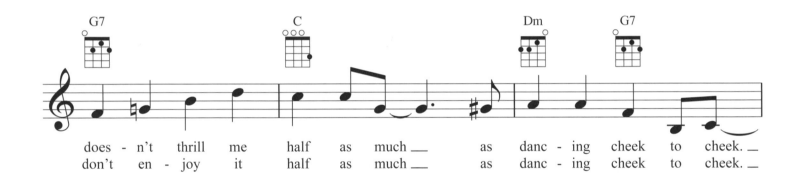

does - n't thrill me half as much ___ as danc - ing cheek to cheek. ___
don't en - joy it half as much ___ as danc - ing cheek to cheek. ___

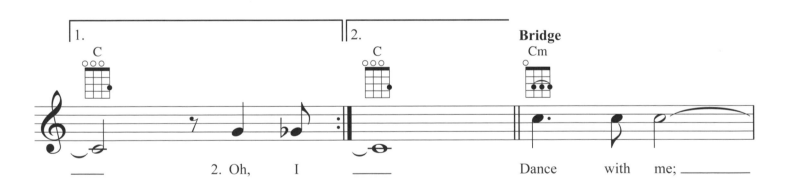

1.   2.   Bridge

2. Oh, I   Dance with me; ___

___ I want my arm a - bout you. ___ The charm a - bout you ___

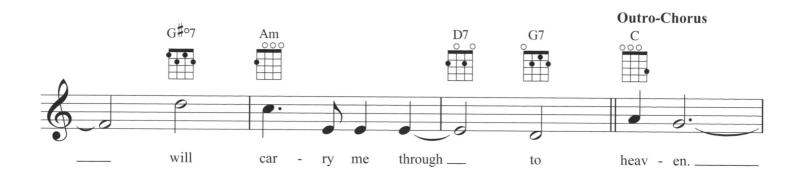

will car - ry me through ___ to heav - en. ___

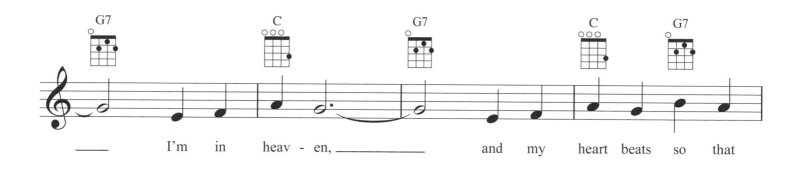

___ I'm in heav - en, ___ and my heart beats so that

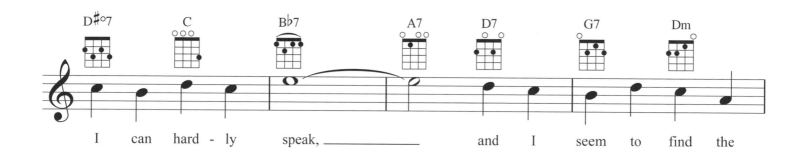

I can hard - ly speak, ___ and I seem to find the

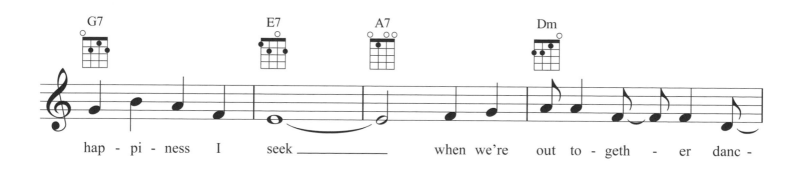

hap - pi - ness I seek ___ when we're out to - geth - er danc -

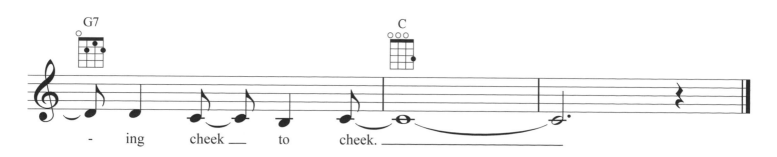

- ing cheek ___ to cheek. ___

Can't Help Lovin' Dat Man

from SHOW BOAT
Lyrics by Oscar Hammerstein II
Music by Jerome Kern

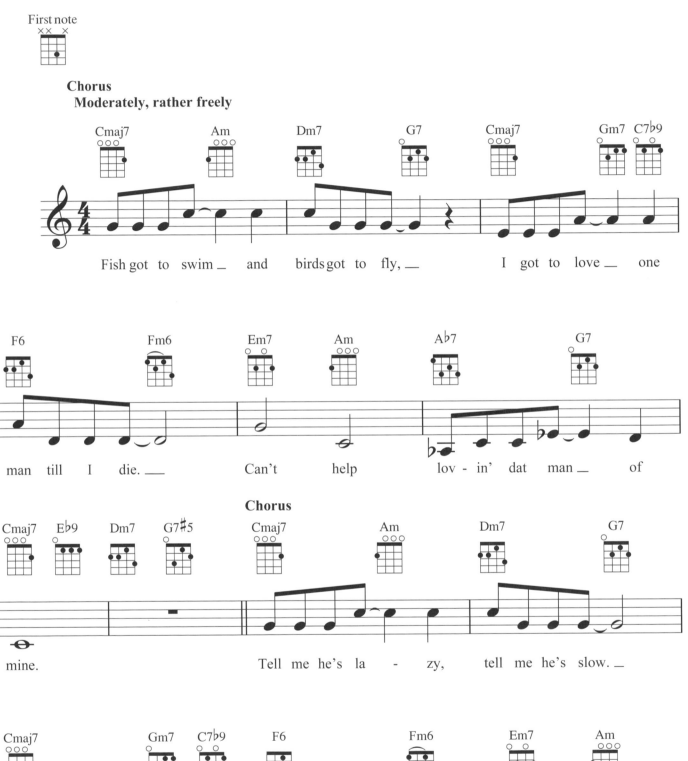

Chorus
Moderately, rather freely

Fish got to swim _ and birds got to fly, _ I got to love _ one

man till I die. _ Can't help lov - in' dat man _ of

Chorus

mine. Tell me he's la - zy, tell me he's slow. _

Tell me I'm cra - zy, may - be I know. _ Can't help

Change Partners

from the RKO Radio Motion Picture CAREFREE
Words and Music by Irving Berlin

you're a - lone, _____ I'll tell the

wait - er to tell him he's want - ed on the tel - e - phone.

Outro-Verse

You've been locked _____ in his arms _____

ev - er since _____ heav - en knows when. _____ Won't you

change part - ners, and then _____ you may

nev - er want _ to change _ part - ners a - gain. _____

Come Fly with Me

Words by Sammy Cahn
Music by James Van Heusen

First note

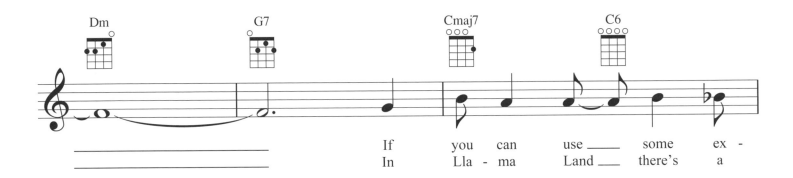

1. Come fly with me! ___ Let's fly! ___ Let's fly ___ a - way! _
(2.) fly with me! ___ Let's float ___ down to ___ Pe - ru! ___

___

If you can use ___ some ex -
In Lla - ma Land ___ there's a

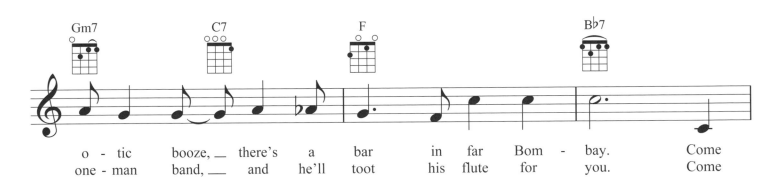

o - tic booze, _ there's a bar in far Bom - bay. Come
one - man band, _ and he'll toot his flute for you. Come

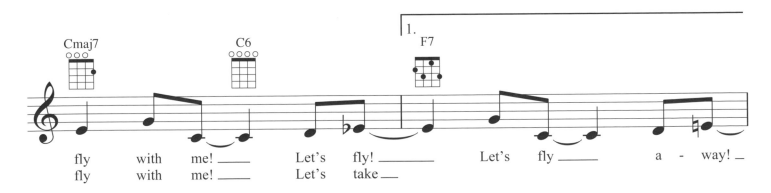

fly with me! ___ Let's fly! ___ Let's fly ___ a - way! ___
fly with me! ___ Let's take ___

Everything's Coming Up Roses

from GYPSY
Lyrics by Stephen Sondheim
Music by Jule Styne

Bridge

Now's our _____ inn - ing, _____ stand the world on its ear! _____ Set it _____ spin - ning; _____ that - 'll be just the be - gin - ning! _____ 3. Cur - tain up, _____ light the lights. _____ We got noth - ing to hit _____ but the heights! _____ We'll be swell, _____

Outro

_____ We'll be great! _____ I can tell, _____

_____ just you wait! _____ That luck - y

star I talk a - bout is due! _____

_____ Hon - ey, ev - 'ry - thing's

com - ing _____ up ros - es _____ for

me and _____ for you. _____

Come Rain or Come Shine

from ST. LOUIS WOMAN
Words by Johnny Mercer
Music by Harold Arlen

Do Nothin' till You Hear from Me

Words and Music by Duke Ellington and Bob Russell

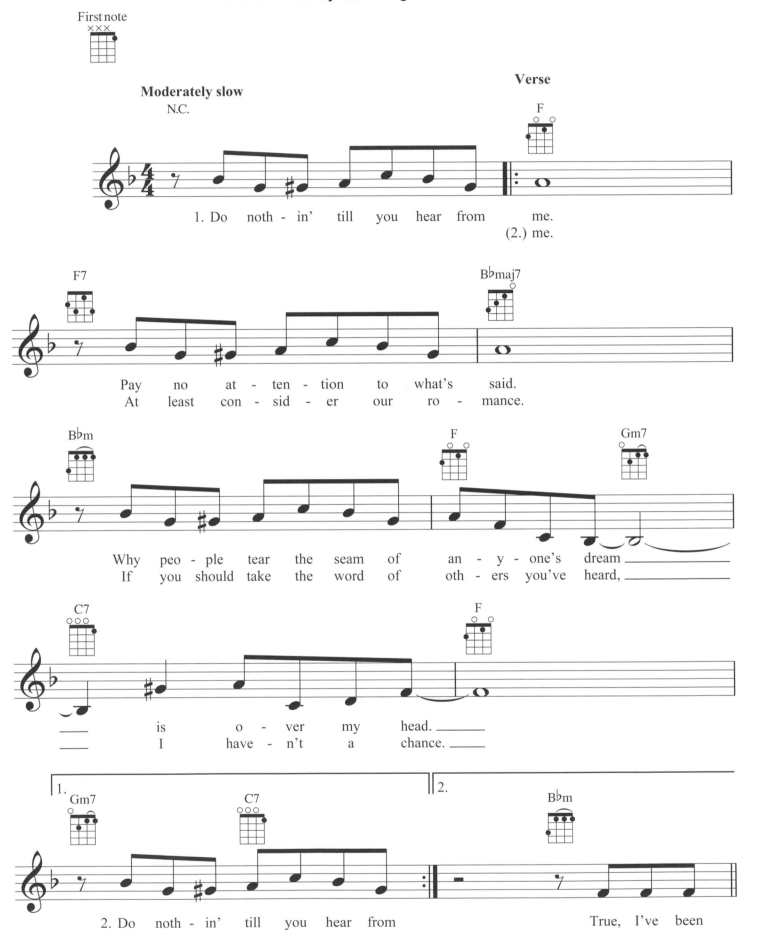

Bridge

seen with some-one new, __ but does that mean

that I'm un - true? __ When we're a - part, _____ the

words in my heart __ re - veal how I feel __ a - bout you. __

Outro-Verse

__ Some kiss may cloud my mem-o - ry, and oth - er arms may hold a

thrill, but please do noth-in' till you hear it from me, _____

__ and you nev - er will. _____

Don't Blame Me

Words by Dorothy Fields
Music by Jimmy McHugh

First note

Verse
Moderately

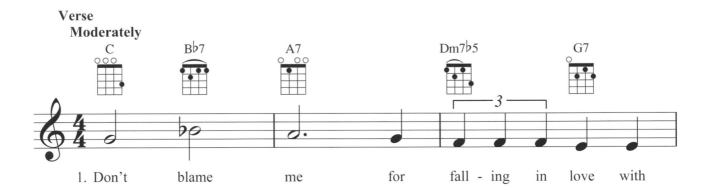

1. Don't blame me for fall-ing in love with

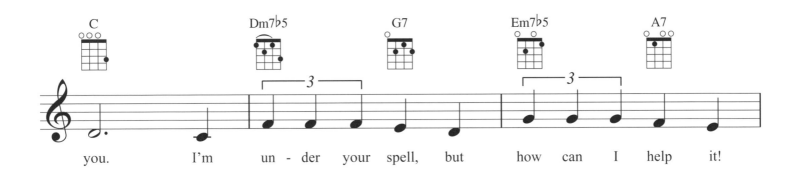

you. I'm un-der your spell, but how can I help it!

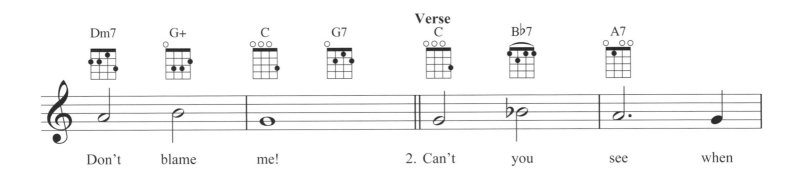

Don't blame me! 2. Can't you see when

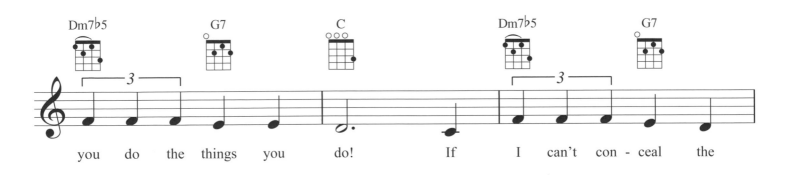

you do the things you do! If I can't con-ceal the

Don't Get Around Much Anymore

Words and Music by Duke Ellington and Bob Russell

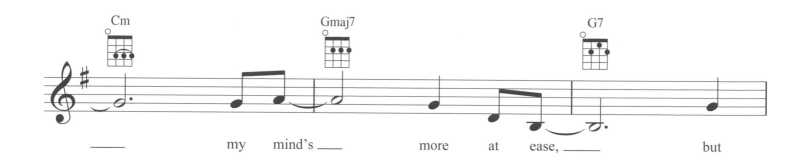

my mind's ___ more at ease, ___ but

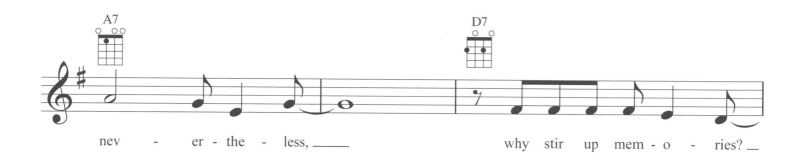

nev - er - the - less, ___ why stir up mem - o - ries? ___

Outro-Verse

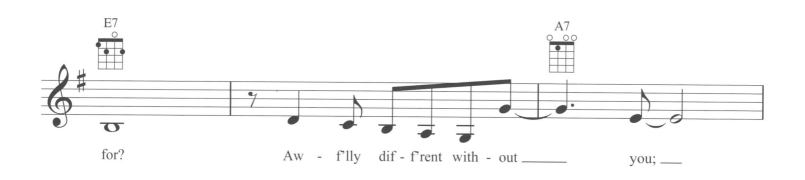

___ Been in - vit - ed on dates; might have gone, but what

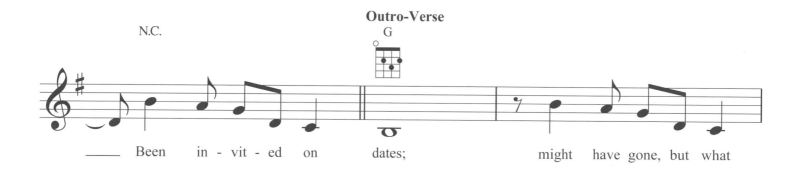

for? Aw - f'lly dif - f'rent with - out ___ you; ___

don't get a - round much an - y - more.

Dream a Little Dream of Me

Words by Gus Kahn
Music by Wilbur Schwandt and Fabian Andree

Outro-Verse

Sweet dreams till sun - beams find you,

sweet dreams that leave all wor - ries be - hind you,

but in your dreams what - ev - er they be,

dream a lit - tle dream of me.

Easy Living

Theme from the Paramount Picture EASY LIVING
Words and Music by Leo Robin and Ralph Rainger

First note

Verse
Moderately, dreamily

1. Liv - ing   for you   is eas - y   liv - ing.   It's
(2.) nev - er   re - gret   the years I'm giv - ing. They're

eas - y   to live   when you're in love.   And I'm so   in love,   there's
eas - y   to give,   when you're in love.   I'm hap - py   to do   what -

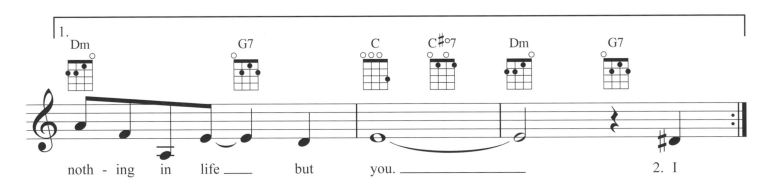

1.
noth - ing   in life ___ but   you. ___   2. I

2.
ev - er   I do ___ for   you. ___   **Bridge**   For   you,

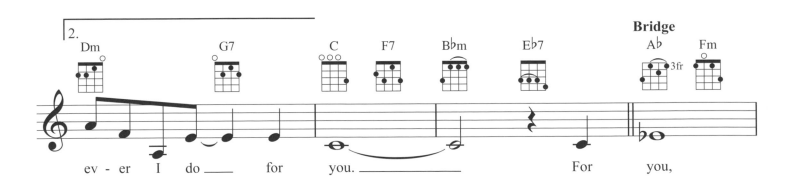

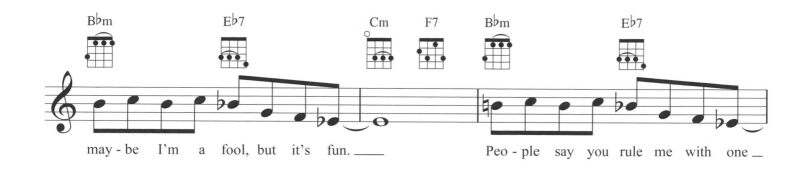

may - be I'm a fool, but it's fun. ____ Peo - ple say you rule me with one __

____ wave of your hand; ___ dar - ling, it's grand. ___ They

Outro-Verse

just don't un - der - stand. Liv - ing for you is eas - y liv - ing. It's

eas - y to live when you're in love. And I'm so in love, there's

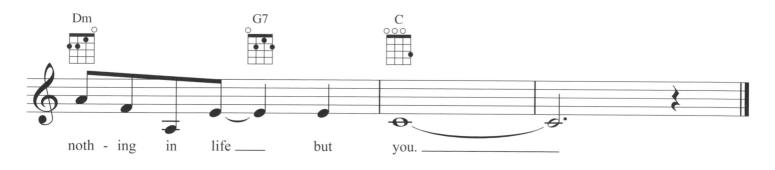

noth - ing in life ___ but you. ____

A Fine Romance

from SWING TIME
Words by Dorothy Fields
Music by Jerome Kern

First note

Verse
Moderately, in 2

1. A fine ro - mance with no
(2.) fine ro - mance, my good

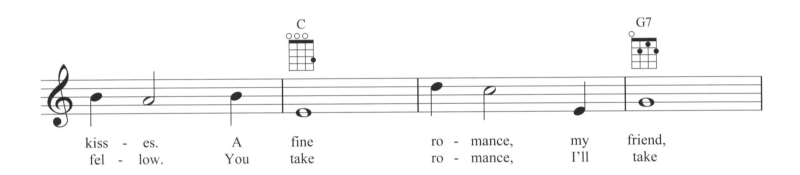

kiss - es. A fine ro - mance, my friend,
fel - low. You take ro - mance, I'll take

this is! We should be like a cou - ple of hot to -
jel - lo! You're calm - er than the seal in the Arc - tic

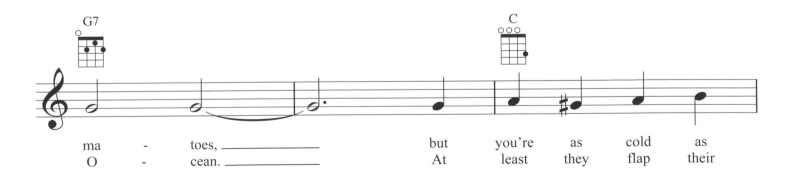

ma - toes, _____ but you're as cold as
O - cean. _____ At least they flap their

For You, For Me, For Evermore

Music and Lyrics by George Gershwin and Ira Gershwin

First note

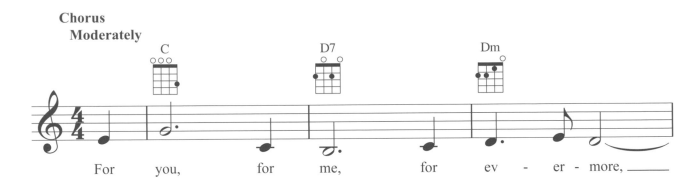

Chorus
Moderately

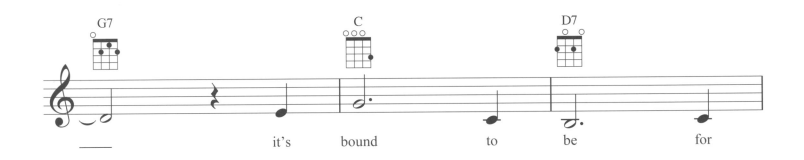

For you, for me, for ev - er - more, _____

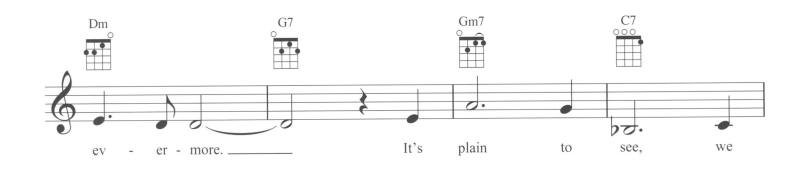

_____ it's bound to be for

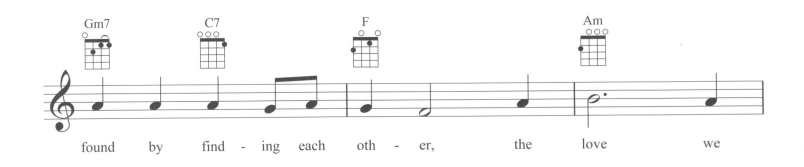

ev - er - more. _____ It's plain to see, we

found by find - ing each oth - er, the love we

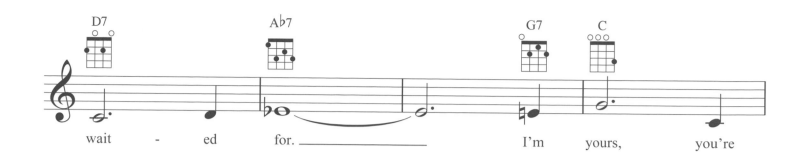

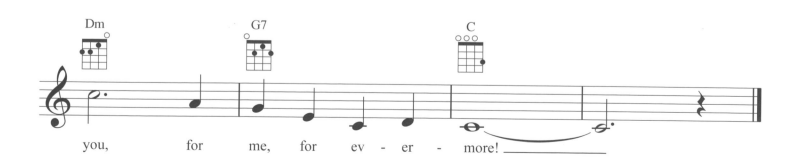

Georgia on My Mind

Words by Stuart Gorrell
Music by Hoagy Carmichael

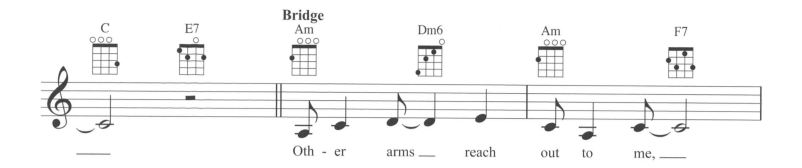

Bridge

Oth - er arms ___ reach out to me, ___

oth - er eyes ___ smile ten - der - ly. ___ Still, in peace - ful

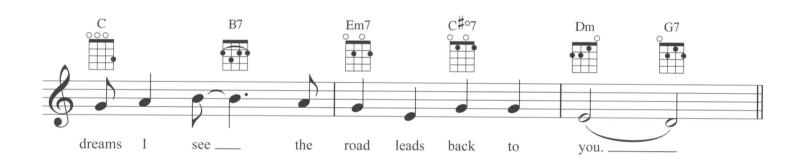

dreams I see ___ the road leads back to you. ___

Outro-Chorus

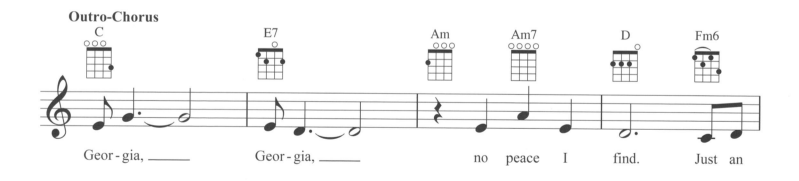

Geor - gia, ___ Geor - gia, ___ no peace I find. Just an

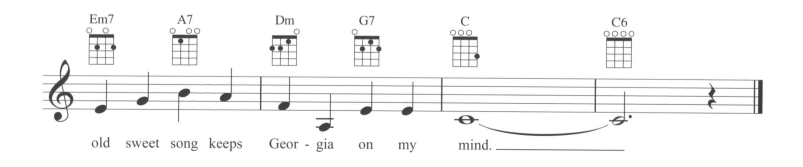

old sweet song keeps Geor - gia on my mind. ___

Here's That Rainy Day

from CARNIVAL IN FLANDERS
Words by Johnny Burke
Music by Jimmy Van Heusen

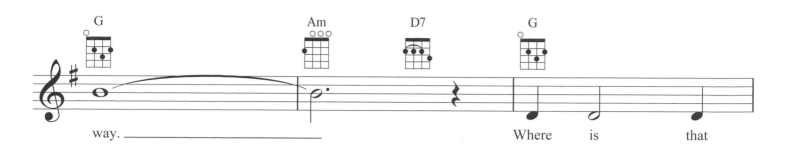

way. _____ Where is that

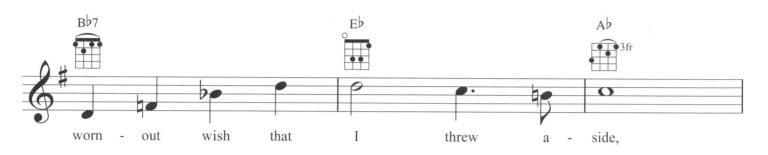

worn - out wish that I threw a - side,

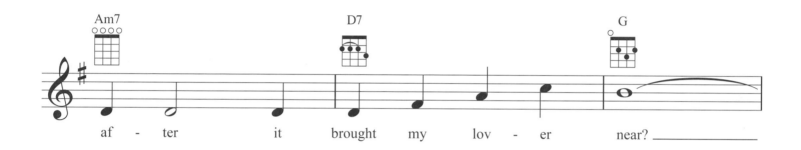

af - ter it brought my lov - er near? _____

_____ Fun - ny how love be - comes a

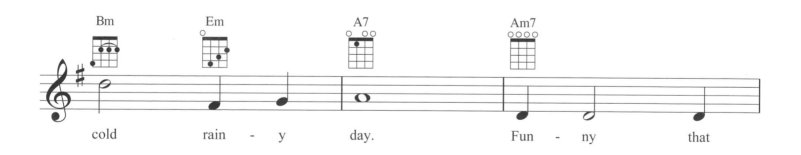

cold rain - y day. Fun - ny that

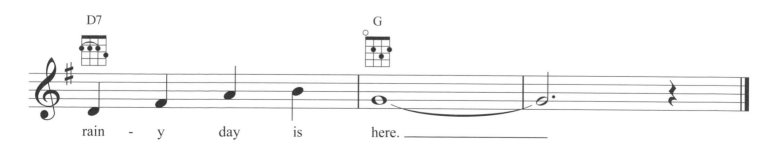

rain - y day is here. _____

Honeysuckle Rose

from AIN'T MISBEHAVIN'
from TIN PAN ALLEY
Words by Andy Razaf
Music by Thomas "Fats" Waller

How Are Things in Glocca Morra

from FINIAN'S RAINBOW
Words by E.Y. "Yip" Harburg
Music by Burton Lane

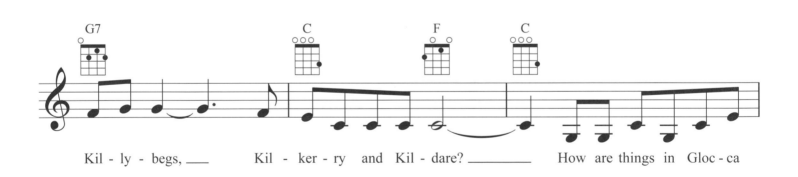

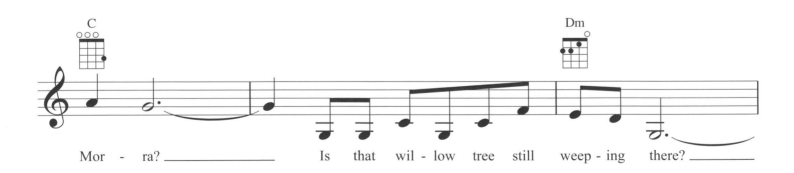

I Can Dream, Can't I?

from RIGHT THIS WAY
Words by Irving Kahal
Music by Sammy Fain

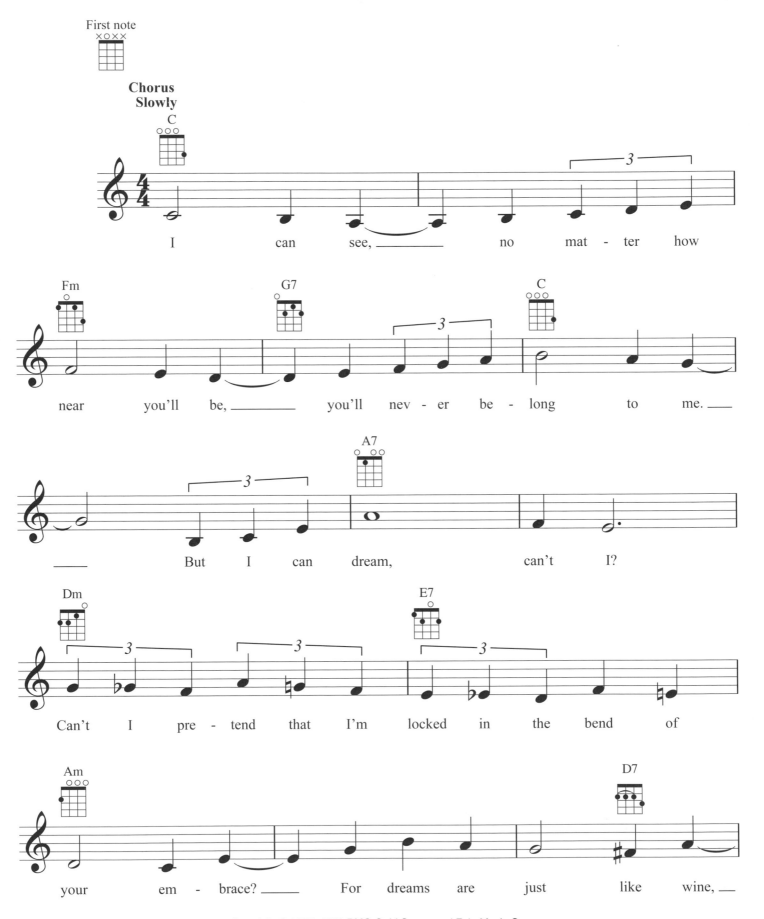

and I am drunk with mine. _____

I'm a - ware _____ my heart is a sad af - fair; _____

_____ there's much dis - il - lu - sion there. _____ But I can

dream, can't I? Can't I a - dore you al -

though we are o - ceans a - part? I can't make you o - pen your

heart, but I can dream, can't I?

I Can't Get Started

from ZIEGFELD FOLLIES
Words by Ira Gershwin
Music by Vernon Duke

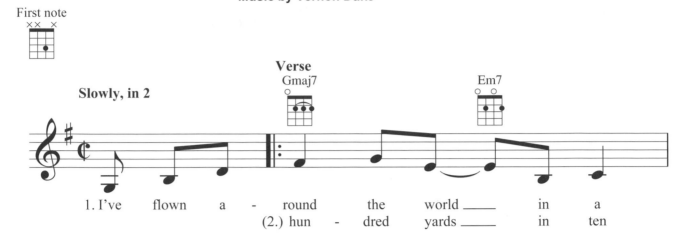

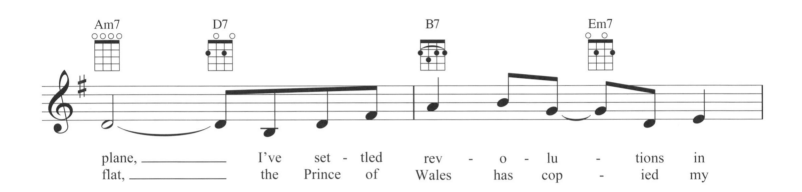

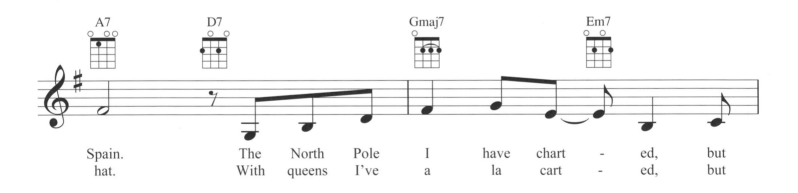

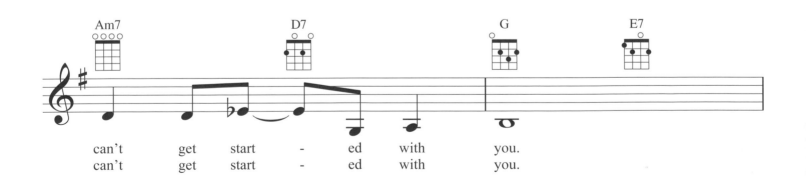

A - round a golf course I'm _____ un - der
The lead - ing tail - ors fol - low my

par, _____ and all the mov - ies want _____ me to
styles, _____ and tooth - paste ads all fea - ture my

star. I've got a house, a show - place, but
smiles. The As - tor - bilts I vis - it; but

I get no _____ place with you. You're so su -
say, what is _____ it with you? When we first

Bridge

preme, lyr - ics I write _____ of you scheme
met, how you e - lat - ed me! Pet,

87

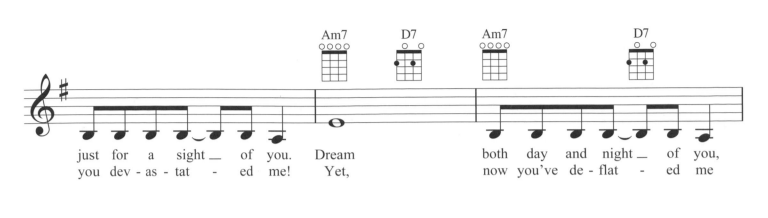

just for a sight __ of you. Dream
you dev - as - tat - ed me! Yet,

both day and night __ of you,
now you've de - flat - ed me

Outro-Verse

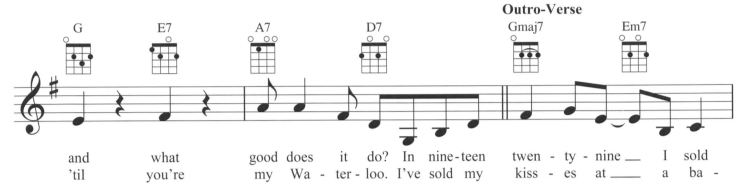

and what good does it do? In nine - teen twen - ty - nine __ I sold
'til you're my Wa - ter - loo. I've sold my kiss - es at ___ a ba -

short, _____ in Eng - land I'm pre - sent - ed at court. But you've got
zaar, _____ and af - ter me they've named __ a ci - gar. But late - ly

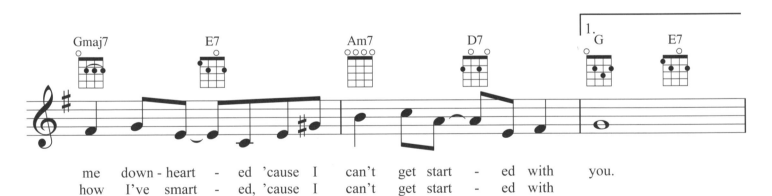

me down - heart - ed 'cause I can't get start - ed with you.
how I've smart - ed, 'cause I can't get start - ed with

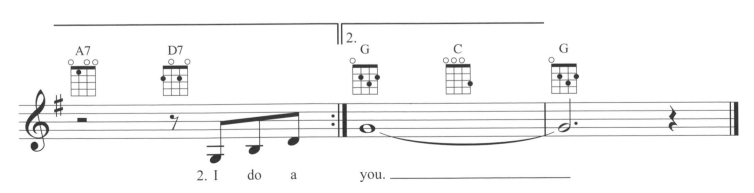

2. I do a you. _____

I Don't Know Why
(I Just Do)

Lyric by Roy Turk
Music by Fred E. Ahlert

I Can't Give You Anything but Love

from BLACKBIRDS OF 1928
Words and Music by Jimmy McHugh and Dorothy Fields

First note

Chorus
Snappy

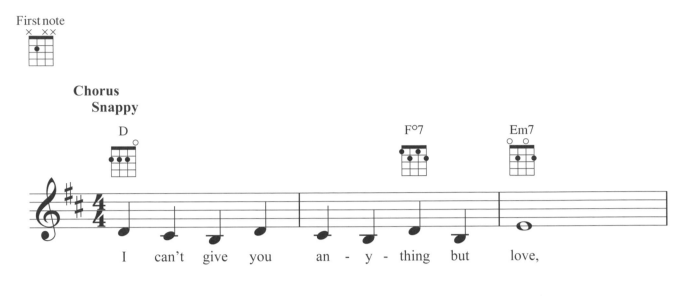

I can't give you an - y - thing but love,

ba - by. That's the on - ly thing I've plen - ty

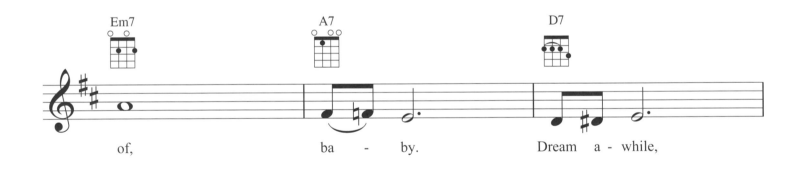

of, ba - by. Dream a - while,

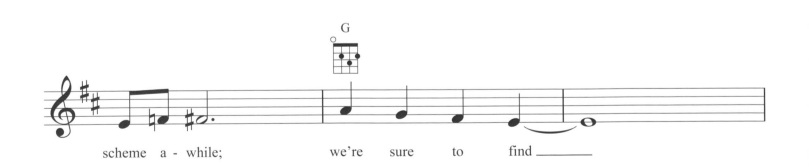

scheme a - while; we're sure to find _____

I Could Have Danced All Night

from MY FAIR LADY
Words by Alan Jay Lerner
Music by Frederick Loewe

I Found a Million Dollar Baby

(In a Five and Ten Cent Store)

from FUNNY LADY

Words and Music by Billy Rose, Mort Dixon and Harry Warren

Bridge

five and ten cent store. She was sell-ing chi-na, _____

_____ and when she made those eyes, _____ I kept buy-ing

chi - na _____ un-til the crowd got wise. _____

Outro-Verse

_____ In-ci-dent-'ly, if you should run in-to a show-er,

just step in-side my cot-tage door and meet the mil-lion dol-lar

ba - by from the five and ten cent store!

I Love My Baby

(My Baby Loves Me)

Words by Bud Green
Music by Harry Warren

First note

Verse
Moderately, in 2

1. I love my ba - by, my ba - by loves me.
2. I love my ba - by, my ba - by loves me.

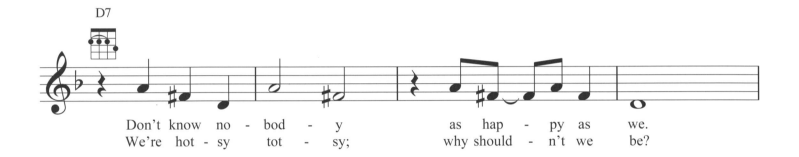

Don't know no - bod - y as hap - py as we.
We're hot - sy tot - sy; why should - n't we be?

She's on - ly twen - ty, and I'm twen - ty - one. ___
She gives me kiss - es, each one is a smack. ___

We nev - er wor - ry; we're just hav - in' fun. ___
But you should hear 'em when I give 'em back. ___

Some - times we quar - rel, and may - be we fight,
She bought a cook - book, she's learn - ing to bake.

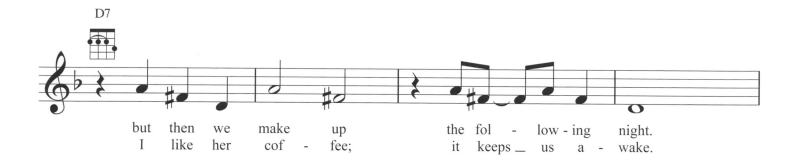

D7

but then we make up the fol - low - ing night.
I like her cof - fee; it keeps — us a - wake.

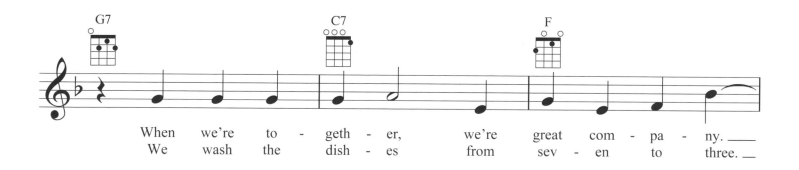

G7   **C7**   **F**

When we're to - geth - er, we're great com - pa - ny. —
We wash the dish - es from sev - en to three. —

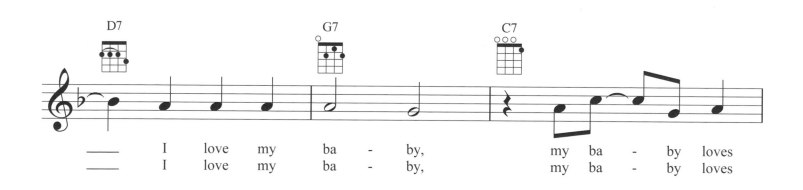

D7   **G7**   **C7**

— I love my ba - by, my ba - by loves
— I love my ba - by, my ba - by loves

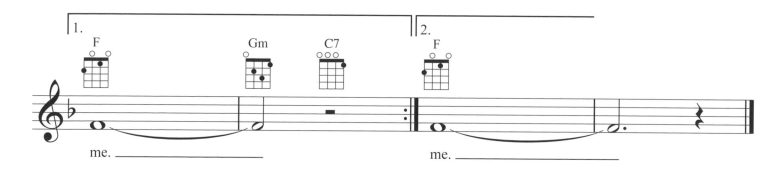

1.
F   **Gm**   **C7**   2. **F**

me. —   me. —

I'll Be Seeing You

from RIGHT THIS WAY
Written by Irving Kahal and Sammy Fain

I'll Get By

(As Long As I Have You)

Lyric by Roy Turk
Music by Fred E. Ahlert

First note

Chorus
Moderately, in 2

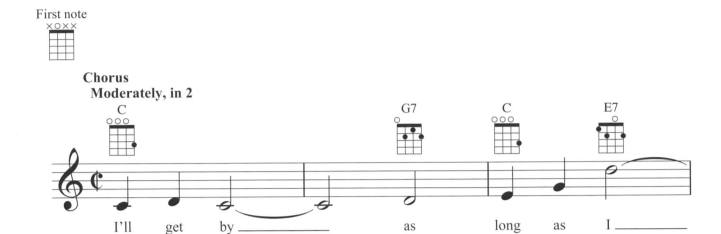

I'll get by _____ as long as I _____

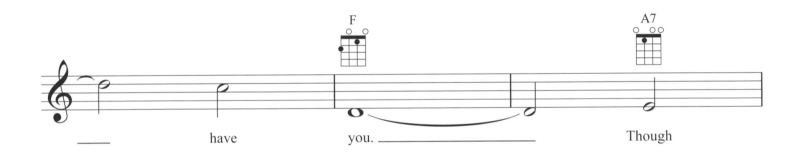

____ have you. _____ Though

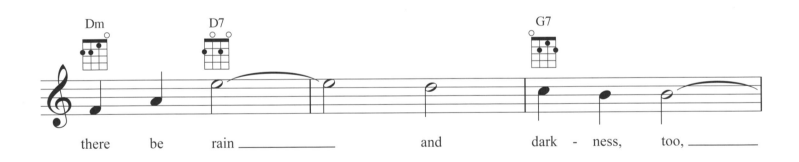

there be rain _____ and dark-ness, too, _____

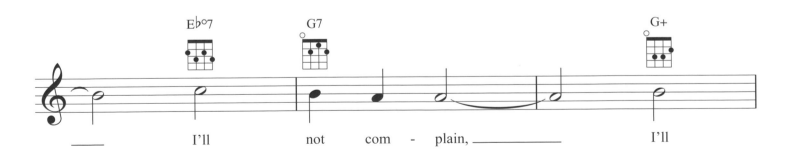

____ I'll not com-plain, _____ I'll

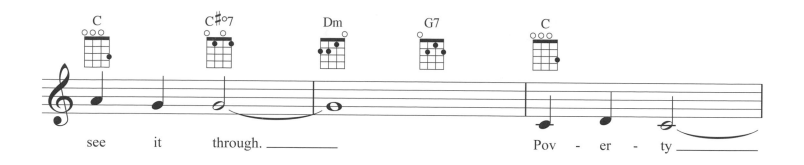

see   it   through. _____   Pov - er - ty _____

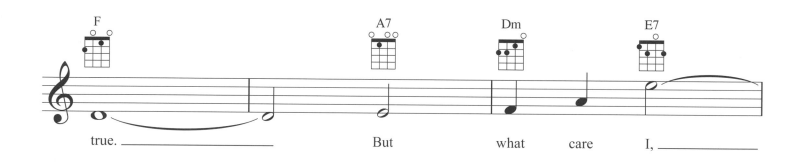

_____   may   come   to   me, _____   that's

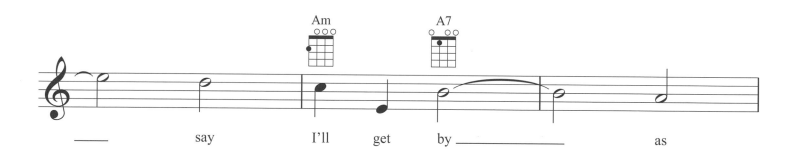

true. _____   But   what   care   I, _____

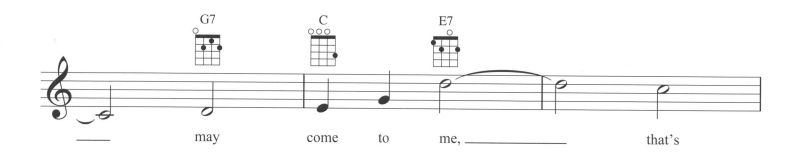

_____   say   I'll   get   by _____   as

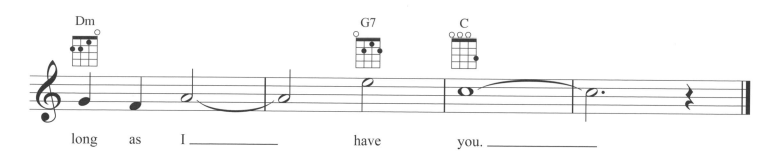

long   as   I _____   have   you. _____

I'm Gonna Sit Right Down and Write Myself a Letter

from AIN'T MISBEHAVIN'
Lyric by Joe Young
Music by Fred E. Ahlert

I'm gon-na sit right down and write my-self a let-ter _____ and make be-lieve it came from you. _____ I'm gon-na write words, oh, so sweet, they're gon-na knock me off my feet. A lot of kiss-es on the bot-tom,

I'm Old Fashioned

from YOU WERE NEVER LOVELIER

Lyrics by Johnny Mercer
Music by Jerome Kern

I've Got the World on a String

Words by Ted Koehler
Music by Harold Arlen

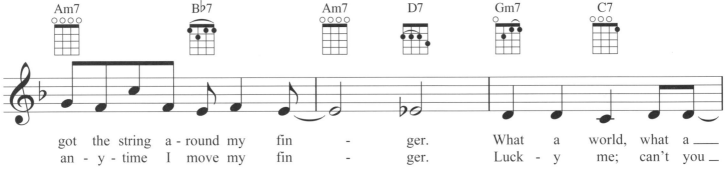

1. I've got the world on a string, __ sit-tin' on a rain-bow,
   song that I sing, __ I can make the rain go

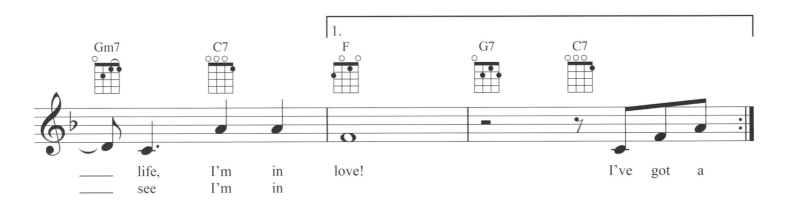

got the string a-round my fin - ger. What a world, what a __
an-y-time I move my fin - ger. Luck-y me; can't you __

__ life, I'm in love! I've got a
__ see I'm in

love? __ Life is a beau-ti-ful thing __

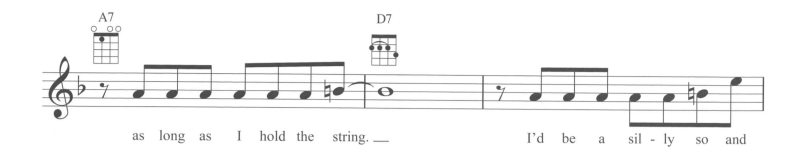

as long as I hold the string. — I'd be a sil - ly so and

so if I should ev - er let go. _____

Outro-Verse

— I've got the world on a string, — sit - tin' on a rain - bow,

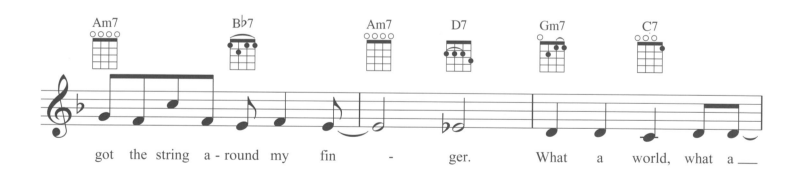

got the string a - round my fin - ger. What a world, what a —

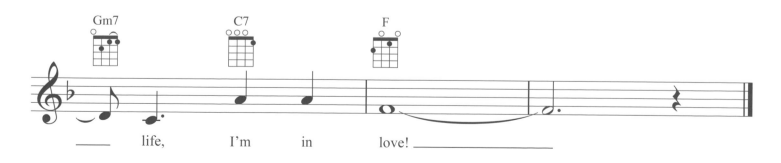

— life, I'm in love! _____

If Ever I Would Leave You

from CAMELOT
Words by Alan Jay Lerner
Music by Frederick Loewe

lus - tre _____ that puts gold to shame! 2. But if I'd ev - er

au - tumn, ____

____ and I must be there. And could I

Bridge

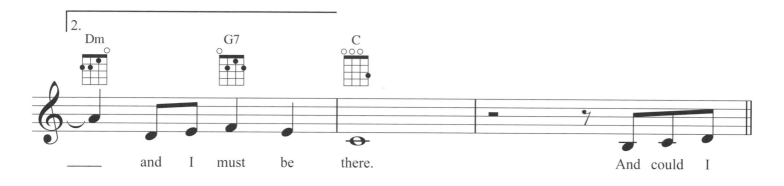

leave you run - ning mer - ri - ly through the snow, _____

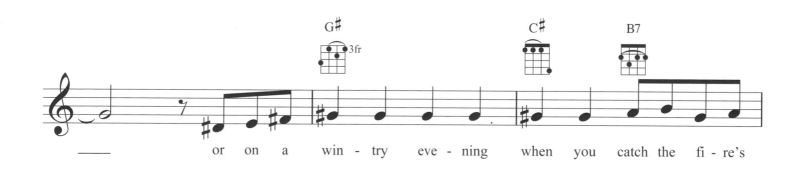

____ or on a win - try eve - ning when you catch the fi - re's

Outro-Verse

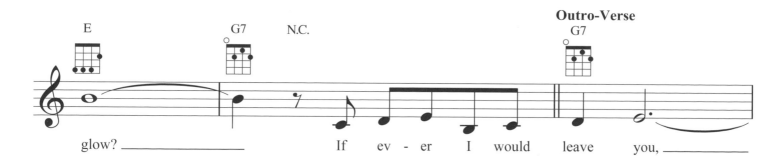

glow? _____ If ev - er I would leave you, _____

109

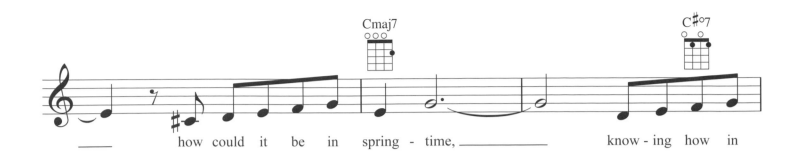

how could it be in spring - time, _____ know - ing how in

spring I'm be - witched by you so? _____

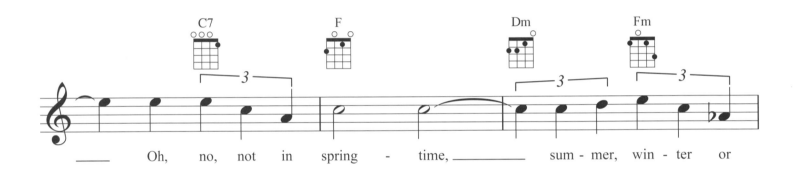

_____ Oh, no, not in spring - time, _____ sum - mer, win - ter or

fall! _____ No, nev - er could I leave you _____

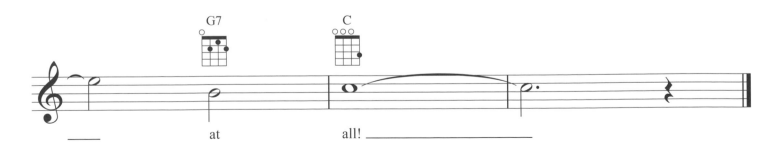

_____ at all! _____

I've Got You Under My Skin

from **BORN TO DANCE**
Words and Music by Cole Porter

If I Were a Bell

from GUYS AND DOLLS
By Frank Loesser

In the Still of the Night

from ROSALIE
from NIGHT AND DAY
Words and Music by Cole Porter

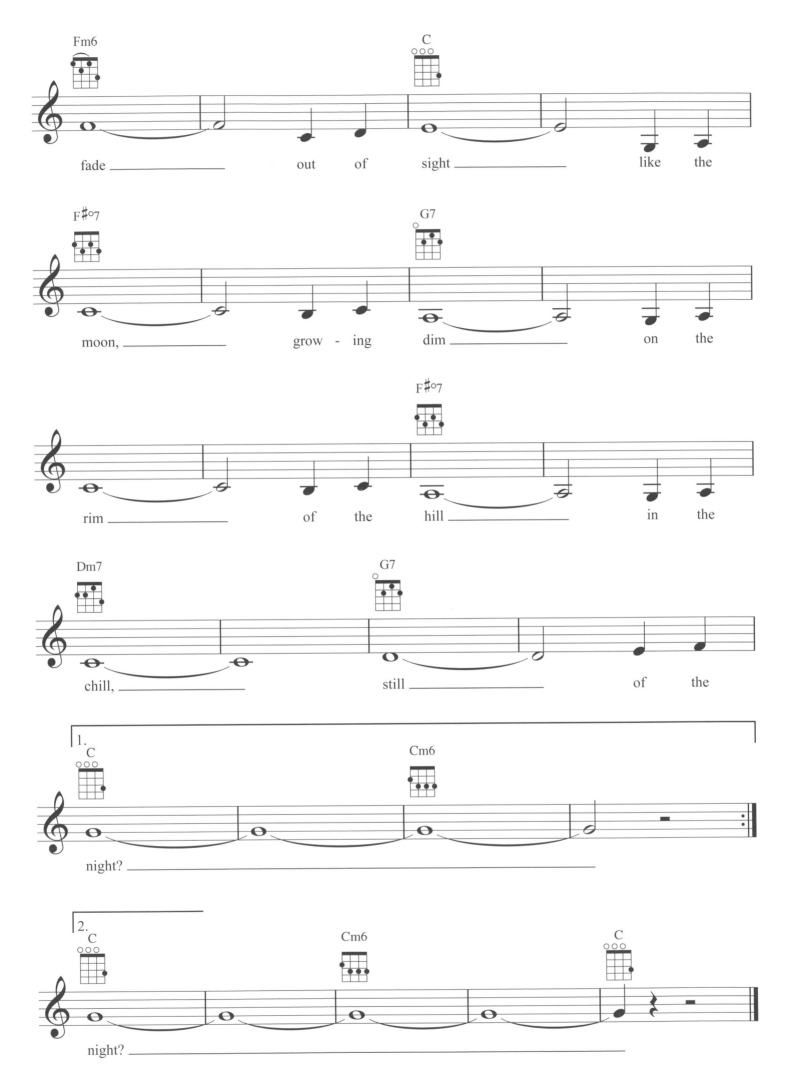

It Might as Well Be Spring

from STATE FAIR
Lyrics by Oscar Hammerstein II
Music by Richard Rodgers

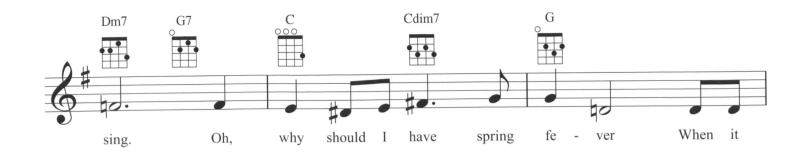

sing.   Oh,   why   should   I   have   spring   fe - ver   When   it

Bridge

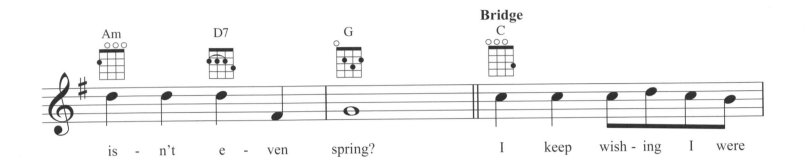

is - n't   e - ven   spring?   I   keep   wish - ing   I   were

some - where   else,   walk - ing   down   a   strange,   new   street,

Hear - ing   words that   I   have   nev - er   heard   from   a   { man girl }   I've   yet   to

Outro-Verse

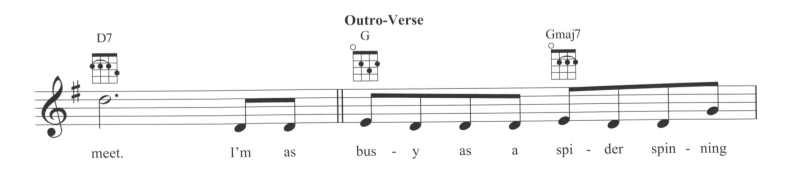

meet.   I'm   as   bus - y   as   a   spi - der   spin - ning

120

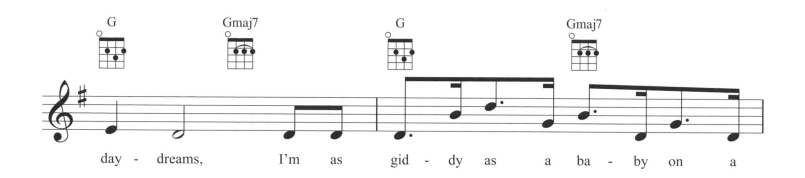

day - dreams, I'm as gid - dy as a ba - by on a

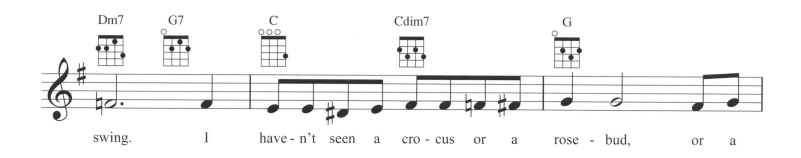

swing. I have - n't seen a cro - cus or a rose - bud, or a

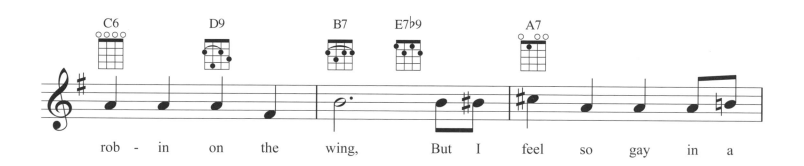

rob - in on the wing, But I feel so gay in a

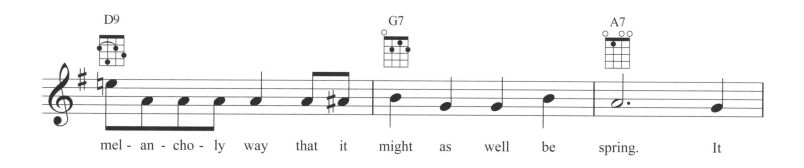

mel - an - cho - ly way that it might as well be spring. It

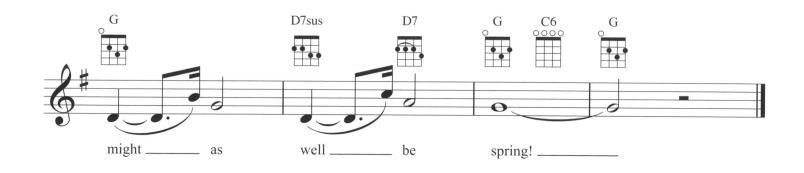

might _____ as well _____ be spring! _____

Isn't It Romantic?

from the Paramount Picture LOVE ME TONIGHT
Words by Lorenz Hart
Music by Richard Rodgers

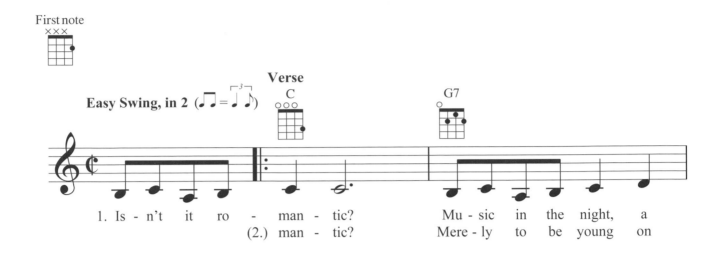

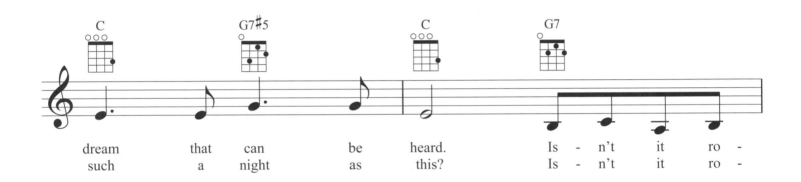

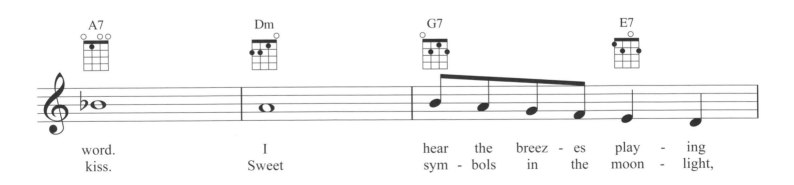

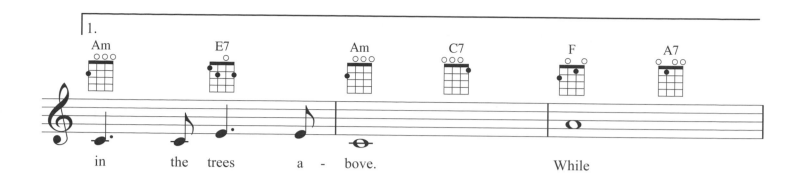

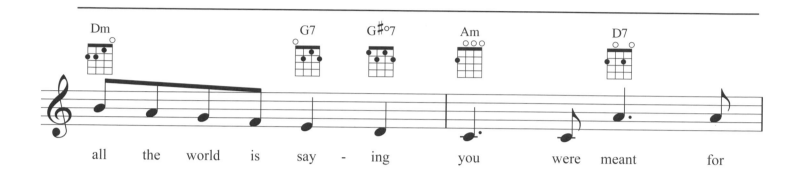

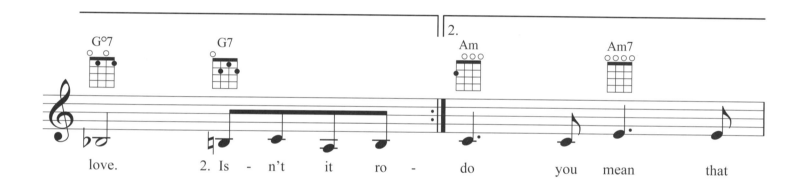

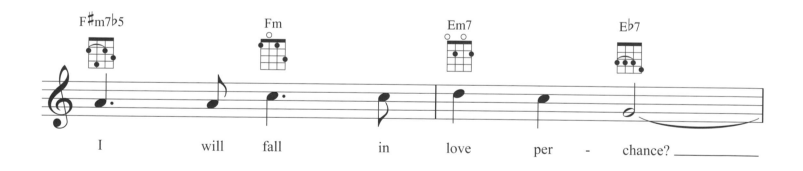

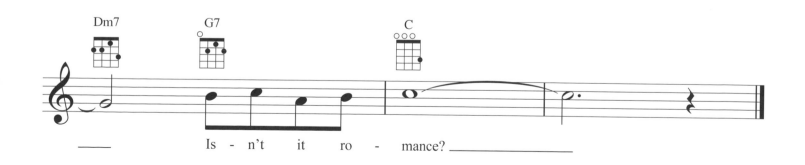

It All Depends on You

from THE SINGING FOOL
Words and Music by B.G. DeSylva, Lew Brown and Ray Henderson

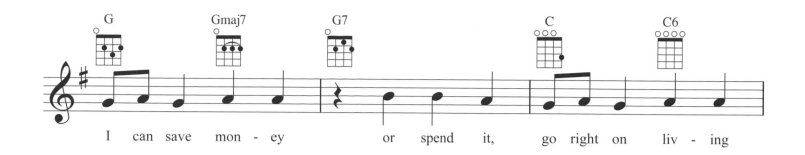

I can save mon - ey or spend it, go right on liv - ing

or end it. You're to blame, hon - ey, for what I

do. _____ I know that I can be beg - gar,

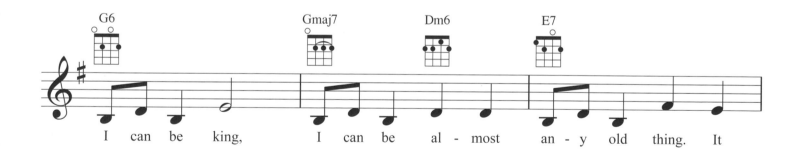

I can be king, I can be al - most an - y old thing. It

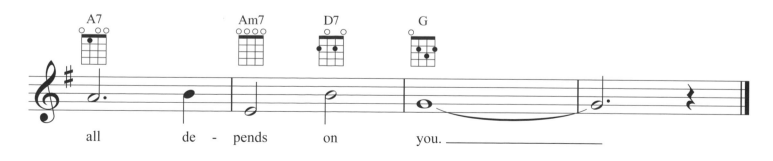

all de - pends on you. _____

It Could Happen to You

from the Paramount Picture AND THE ANGELS SING
Words by Johnny Burke
Music by James Van Heusen

Outro-Chorus

tum - ble. Keep an eye on Spring,

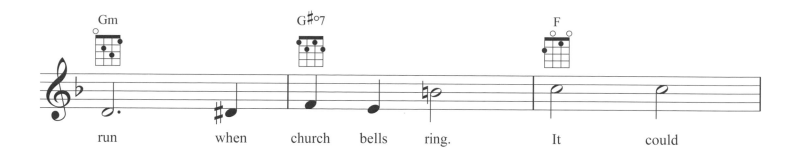

run when church bells ring. It could

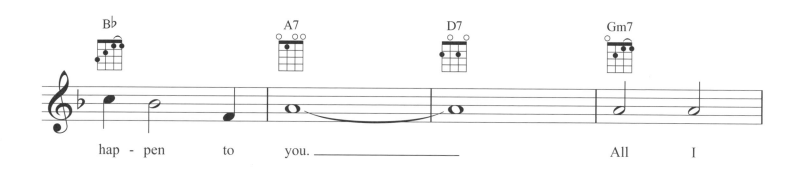

hap - pen to you. _____ All I

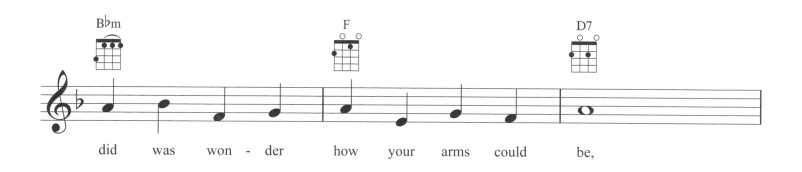

did was won - der how your arms could be,

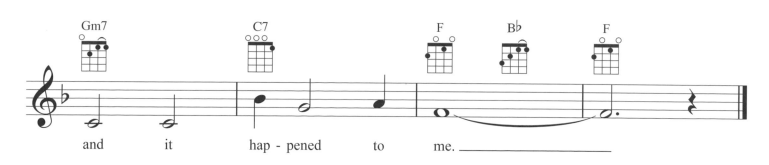

and it hap - pened to me. _____

It's Only a Paper Moon

Lyric by Billy Rose and E.Y. "Yip" Harburg
Music by Harold Arlen

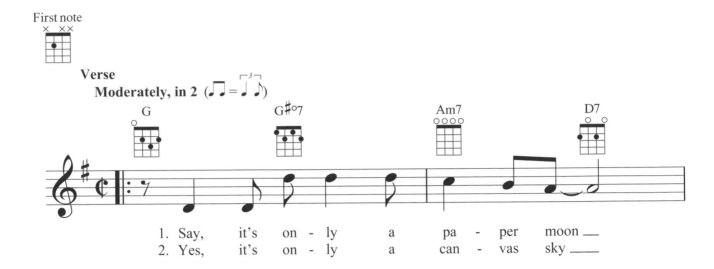

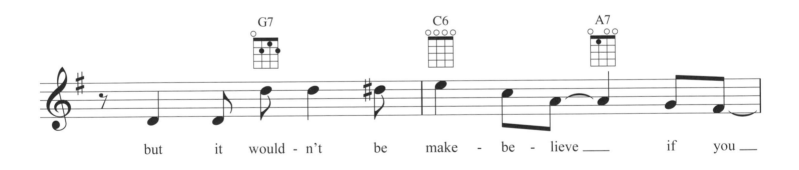

June in January

from the Paramount Picture HERE IS MY HEART
Words and Music by Leo Robin and Ralph Rainger

First note

Verse
Moderately, in 2

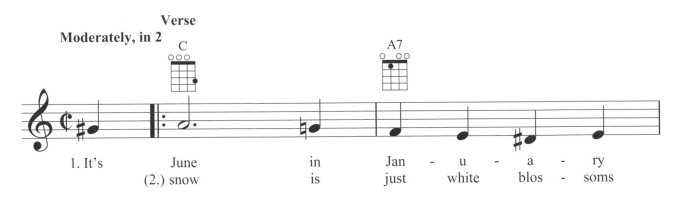

1. It's June in Jan - u - a - ry
(2.) snow is just white blos - soms

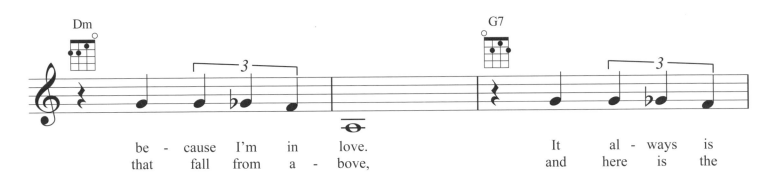

be - cause I'm in love. It al - ways is
that fall from a - bove, and here is the

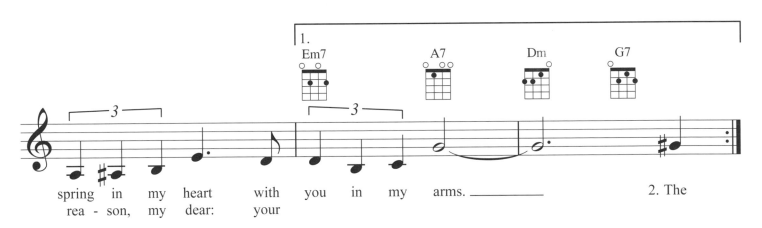

spring in my heart with you in my arms. _____ 2. The
rea - son, my dear: your

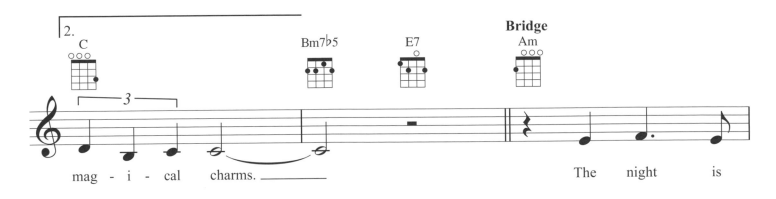

mag - i - cal charms. _____

Bridge

The night is

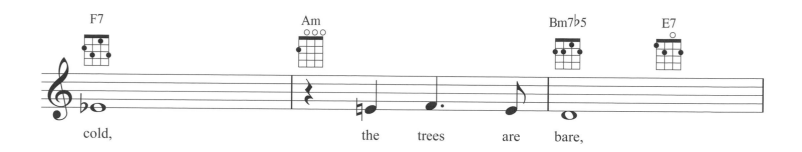

cold,   the trees are bare,

but I can feel the scent of ros - es in the

Outro-Verse

air.   It's June in Jan - u - a - ry

be - cause I'm in love,   but on - ly be -

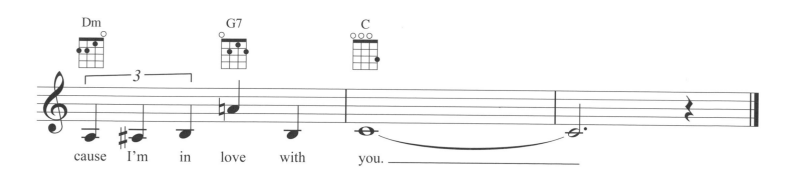

cause I'm in love with you. _____

Just in Time

from BELLS ARE RINGING
Words by Betty Comden and Adolph Green
Music by Jule Styne

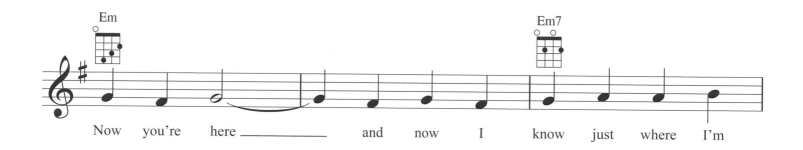

Now you're here _____ and now I know just where I'm

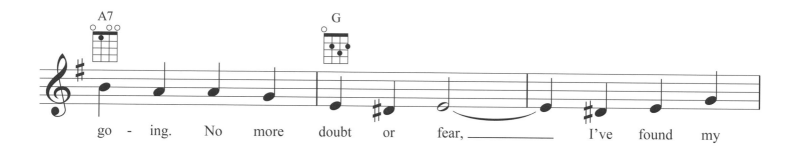

go - ing. No more doubt or fear, _____ I've found my

way. For love came just in time, _____

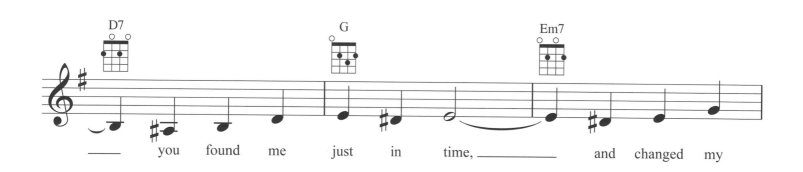

_____ you found me just in time, _____ and changed my

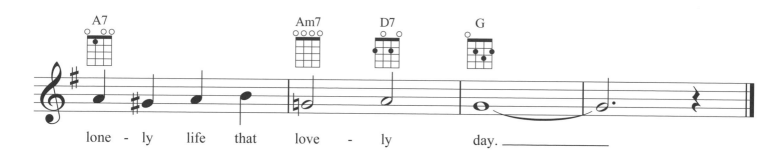

lone - ly life that love - ly day. _____

Let's Fall in Love

Words by Ted Koehler
Music by Harold Arlen

First note

Verse
Moderately bright, in 2

1. Let's fall in love; why should-n't we ____ fall in
2. Let's close our eyes and make our own ____ par - a -

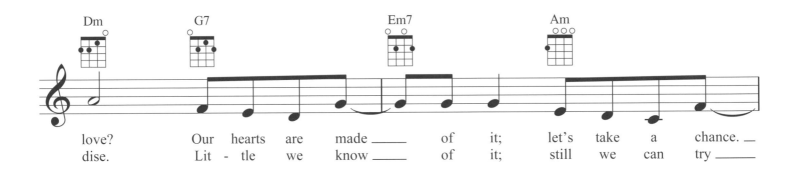

love? Our hearts are made ____ of it; let's take a chance. ____
dise. Lit - tle we know ____ of it; still we can try ____

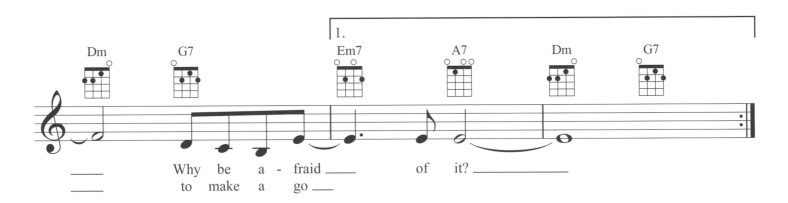

____ Why be a - fraid ____ of it? ____
____ to make a go ____

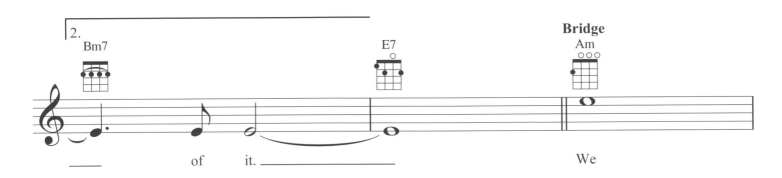

____ of it. ____ We

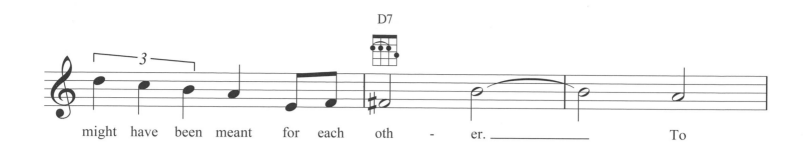

might have been meant for each oth - er. _____ To

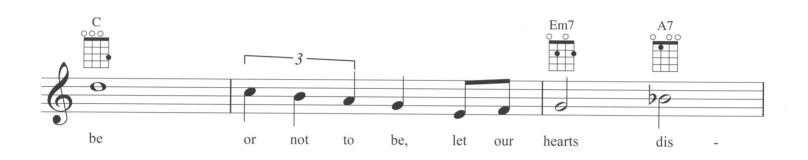

be or not to be, let our hearts dis -

Outro-Verse

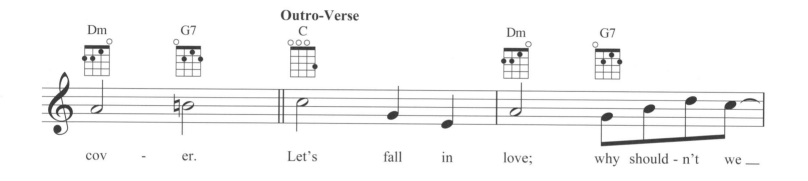

cov - er. Let's fall in love; why should - n't we __

__ fall in love? Now is the time ___ for it while we are

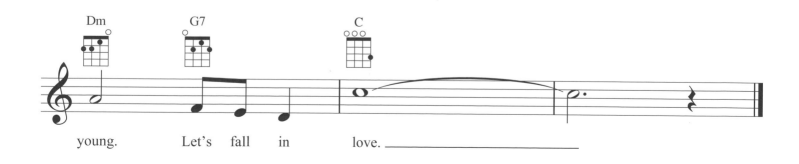

young. Let's fall in love. _____

Little Girl Blue

from JUMBO
Words by Lorenz Hart
Music by Richard Rodgers

Lush Life

Words and Music by Billy Strayhorn

I thought for a while that your poig-nant smile was

tinged with the sad-ness of a great love for me.

Ah, yes, I was wrong, a-gain I was

wrong. Life is lone-ly a-

gain, and on-ly last year ev-'ry-thing seemed so sure. Now

life is aw-ful a-gain; a trough-ful of hearts could on-ly be a

bore. A week in Par - is will ease the bite of it;

all I care is to smile in spite of it.

Outro-Chorus

I'll for - get you, I will, while yet you are still burn ing in - side my

brain. Ro - mance is mush, sti - fling those who strive. __ I'll

live a lush life in some small dive, __ and there I'll be, while I

rot with the rest of those whose lives are lone - ly, too.

Love Letters

Theme from the Paramount Picture LOVE LETTER
Words by Edward Heyman
Music by Victor Young

First note

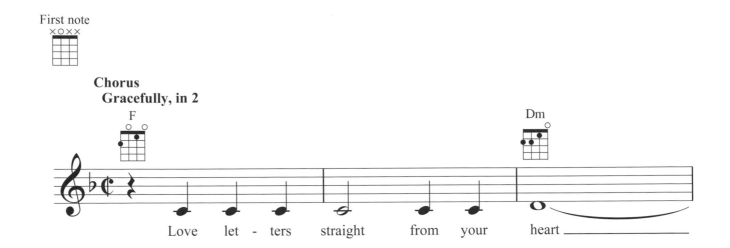

Love let - ters straight from your heart ___

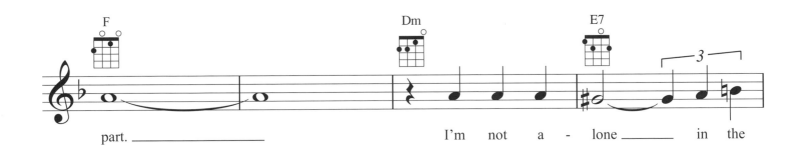

___ keep us so near ___ while a -

part. ___ I'm not a - lone ___ in the

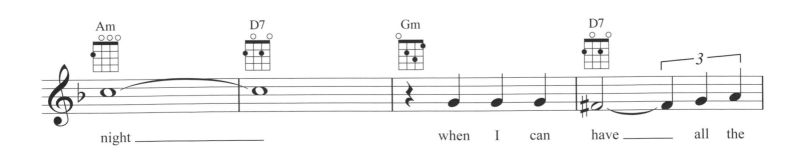

night ___ when I can have ___ all the

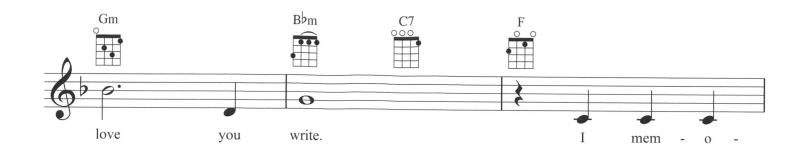

love you write. I mem - o -

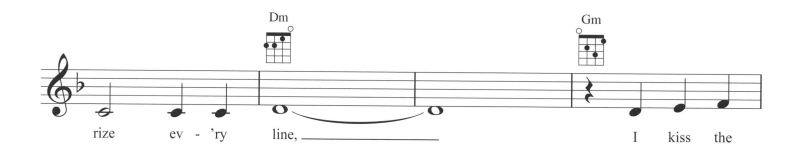

rize ev - 'ry line, _____ I kiss the

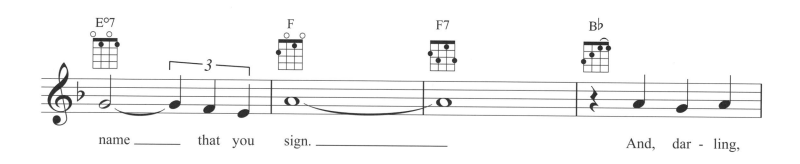

name _____ that you sign. _____ And, dar - ling,

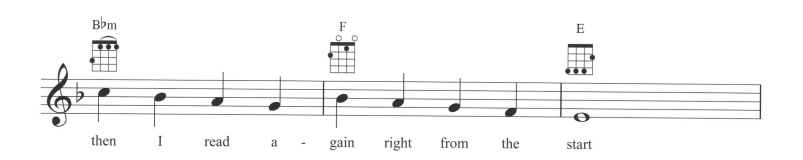

then I read a - gain right from the start

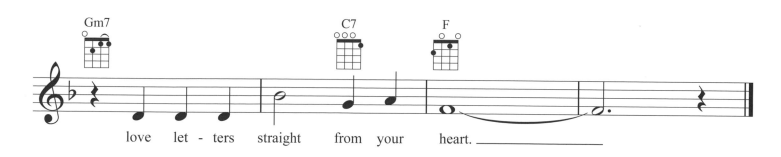

love let - ters straight from your heart. _____

Love Me or Leave Me

from LOVE ME OR LEAVE ME
from WHOOPEE!
Lyrics by Gus Kahn
Music by Walter Donaldson

First note

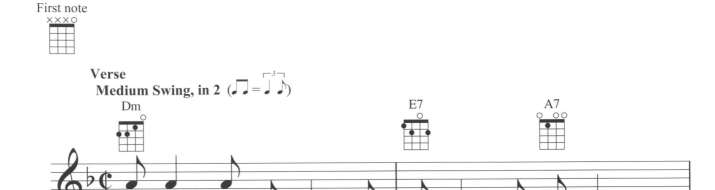

Verse
Medium Swing, in 2

1. Love me or leave me and let me be lone-ly.
(2.) might find the night-time and the right time for kiss-ing, but

You won't be-lieve me, and I love you on-ly. I'd
night-time is my time for just rem-i-nisc-ing. Re-

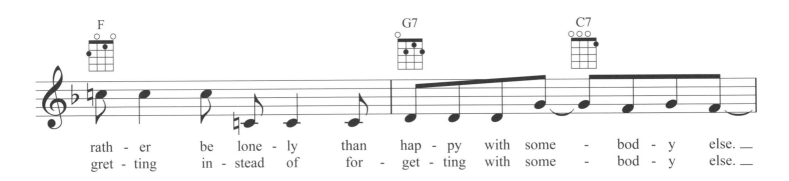

rath-er be lone-ly than hap-py with some-bod-y else. __
gret-ting in-stead of for-get-ting with some-bod-y else. __

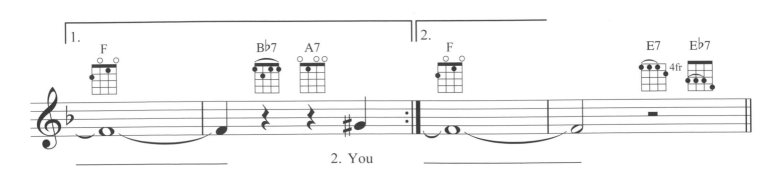

2. You

Makin' Whoopee!

from WHOOPEE!
Lyrics by Gus Kahn
Music by Walter Donaldson

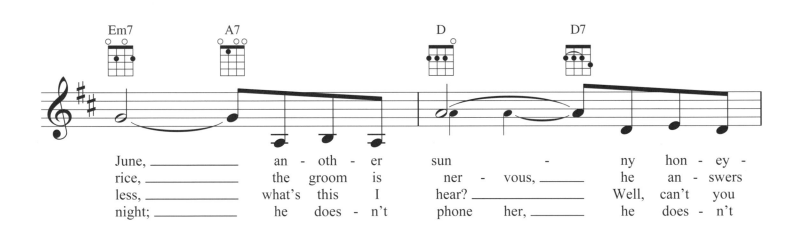

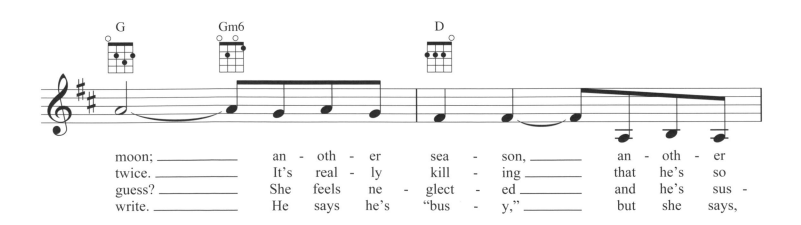

Chorus

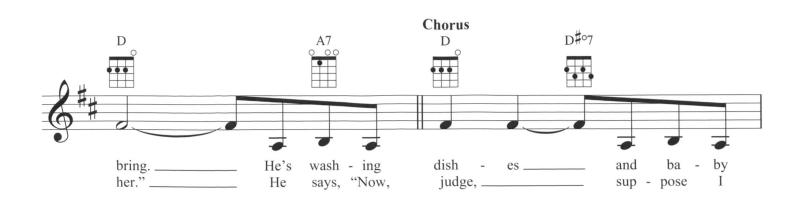

bring. _____ He's wash - ing dish - es _____ and ba - by
her." _____ He says, "Now, judge, _____ sup - pose I

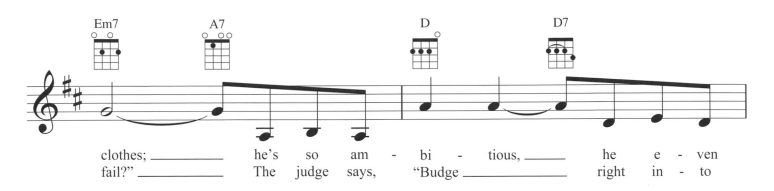

clothes; _____ he's so am - bi - tious, _____ he e - ven
fail?" _____ The judge says, "Budge _____ right in - to

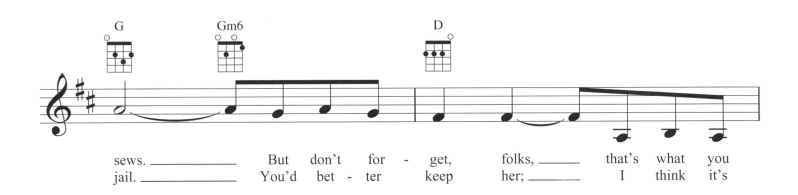

sews. _____ But don't for - get, folks, _____ that's what you
jail. _____ You'd bet - ter keep her; _____ I think it's

To Coda ⊕   *D.S. al Coda*
(with repeat)

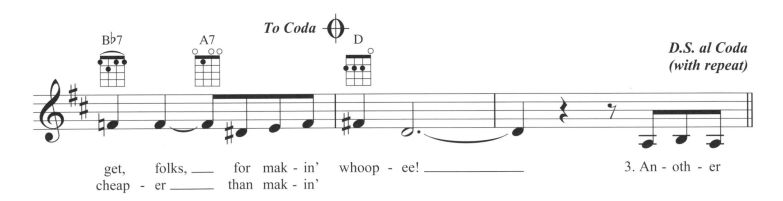

get, folks, ___ for mak - in' whoop - ee! _____   3. An - oth - er
cheap - er _____ than mak - in'

⊕ **Coda**

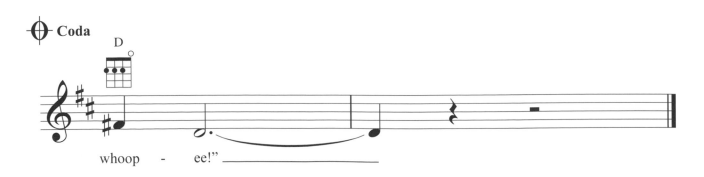

whoop - ee!" _____

146

My Ideal

from the Paramount Picture PLAYBOY OF PARIS
Words by Leo Robin
Music by Richard A. Whiting and Newell Chase

Mona Lisa

from the Paramount Picture CAPTAIN CAREY, U.S.A.
Words and Music by Jay Livingston and Ray Evans

Mo - na Li - sa, Mo - na Li - sa, men have named you. You're so

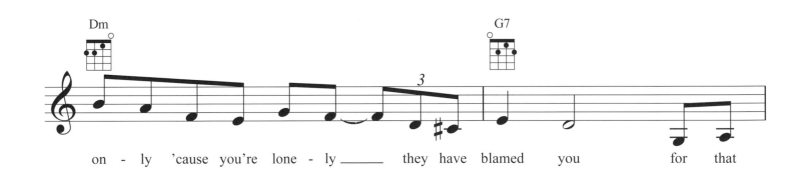

like the la - dy with the mys - tic smile. Is it

on - ly 'cause you're lone - ly _____ they have blamed you for that

Mo - na Li - sa strange - ness _____ in your smile? Do you

smile to tempt a lov - er, _____ Mo - na Li - sa, _____ or is

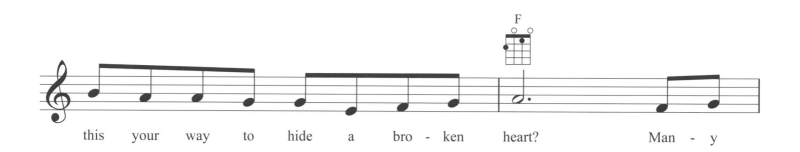

this your way to hide a bro - ken heart? Man - y

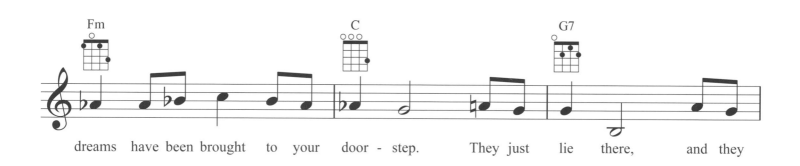

dreams have been brought to your door - step. They just lie there, and they

die there. Are you warm, are you real, Mo - na Li - sa, or just a

cold and lone - ly love - ly work of art? Mo - na art?

Mood Indigo

Words and Music by Duke Ellington, Irving Mills and Albany Bigard

Moon River

from the Paramount Picture BREAKFAST AT TIFFANY'S
Words by Johnny Mercer
Music by Henry Mancini

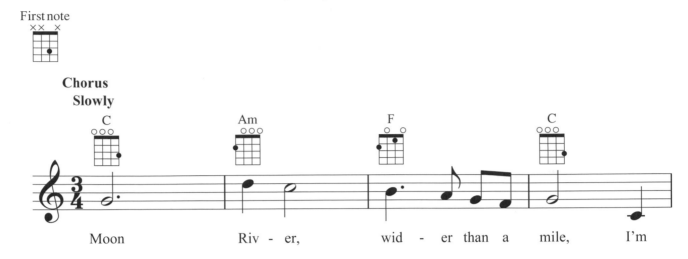

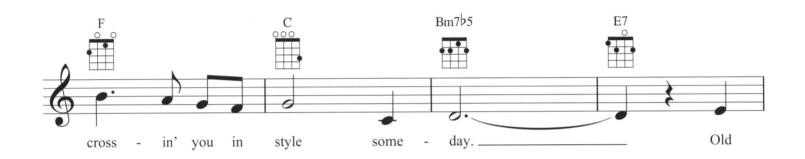

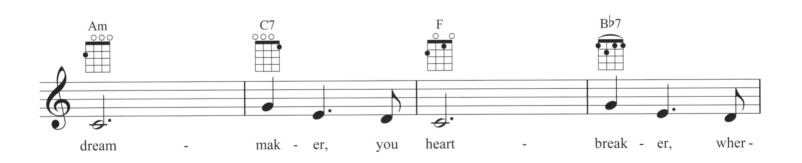

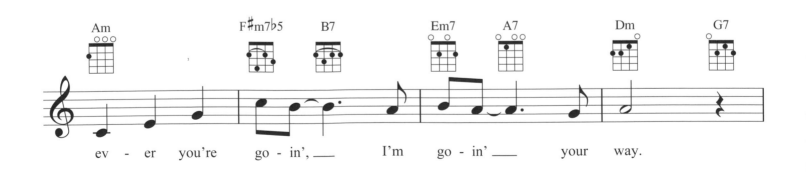

Two drift - ers, off to see the world. There's

such a lot of world to see. _____ We're

af - ter the same rain - bow's

end, wait - in' 'round the bend, my Huck - le - ber - ry

friend, Moon Riv - er _____ and

1. me. _____ 2. me. _____

My Baby Just Cares for Me

from WHOOPEE!
Lyrics by Gus Kahn
Music by Walter Donaldson

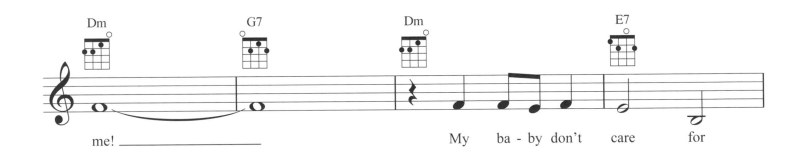

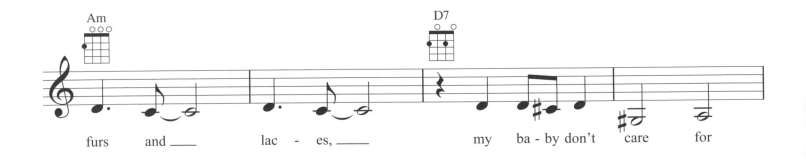

high - toned __ plac - es. __ My ba - by don't

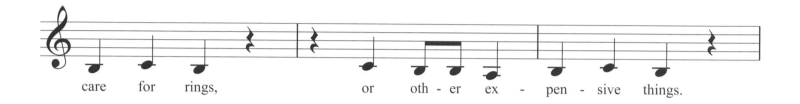

care for rings, or oth - er ex - pen - sive things.

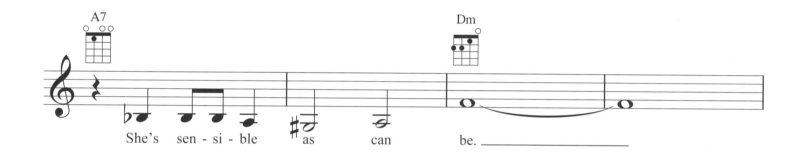

She's sen - si - ble as can be. __

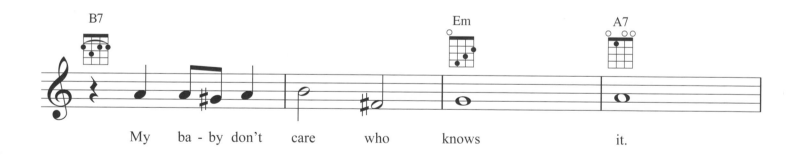

My ba - by don't care who knows it.

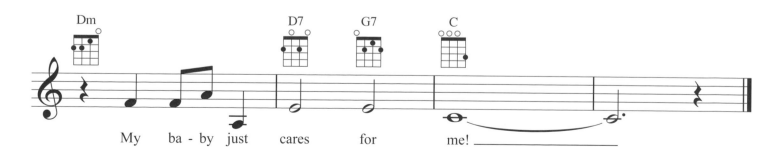

My ba - by just cares for me! __

My Blue Heaven

Lyric by George Whiting
Music by Walter Donaldson

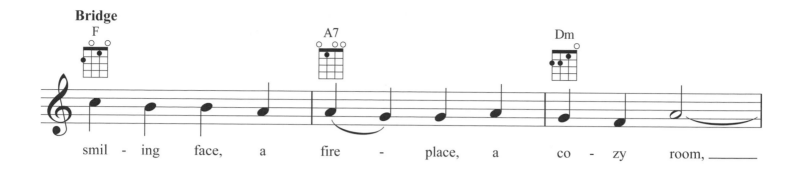

Bridge

smil - ing face, a fire - place, a co - zy room, _____

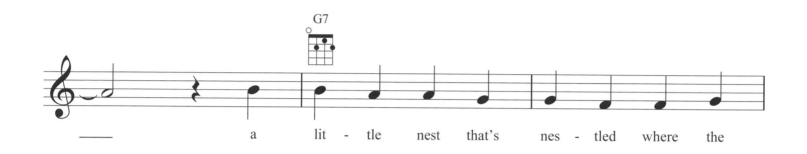

_____ a lit - tle nest that's nes - tled where the

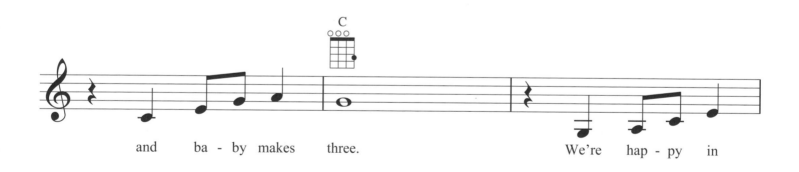

ros - es bloom. 3. Just Mol - lie and me,

Outro-Verse

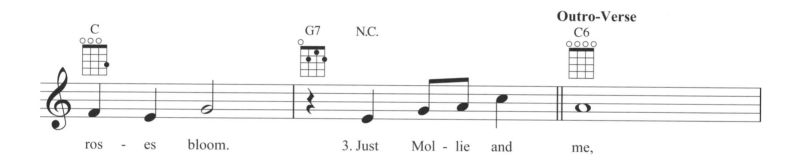

and ba - by makes three. We're hap - py in

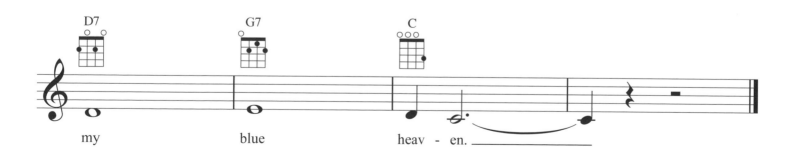

my blue heav - en. _____

My Foolish Heart

from MY FOOLISH HEART
Words by Ned Washington
Music by Victor Young

First note

Verse
Slowly and expressively

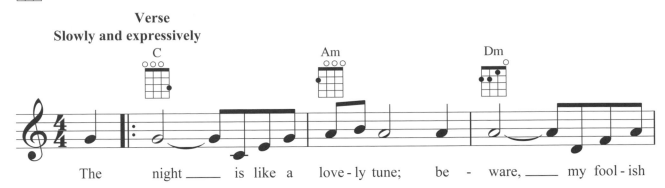

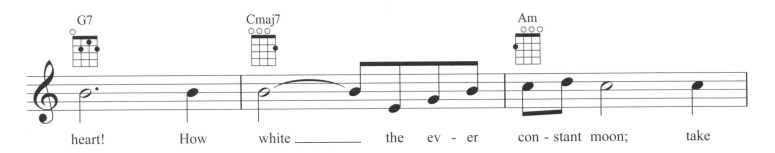

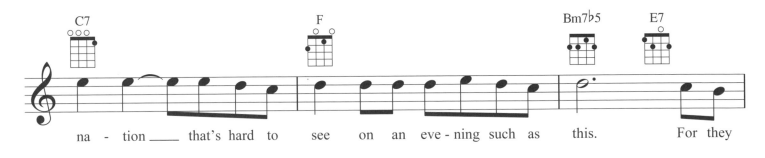

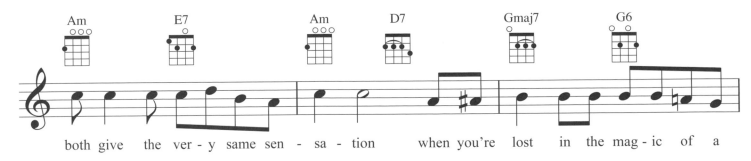

Outro-Verse

kiss. { His Her } lips _____ are much too close to mine; be-

ware, _____ my fool-ish heart! But should _____ our ea-ger

lips com-bine, then let _____ the fire _____ start. For

this time it is-n't fas-ci-na-tion, or a dream that will fade and fall a-

part. It's love, _____ this time it's love, my fool-ish

heart. The heart. _____

My Funny Valentine

from BABES IN ARMS
Words by Lorenz Hart
Music by Richard Rodgers

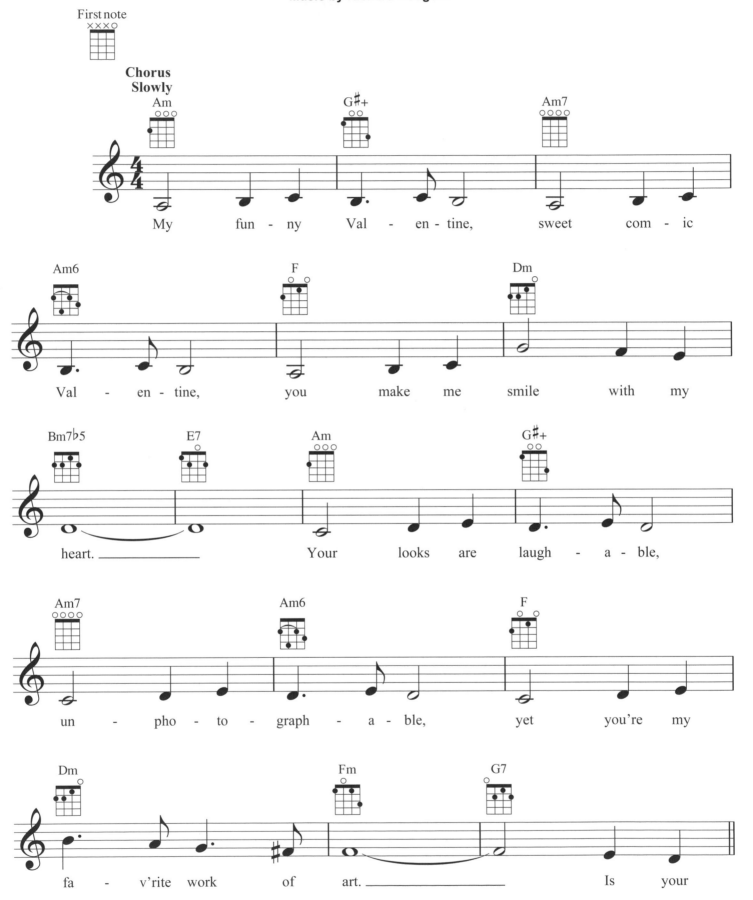

The Nearness of You

from the Paramount Picture ROMANCE IN THE DARK
Words by Ned Washington
Music by Hoagy Carmichael

On a Clear Day
(You Can See Forever)

from ON A CLEAR DAY YOU CAN SEE FOREVER
Words by Alan Jay Lerner
Music by Burton Lane

Outro-Chorus

165

On a Slow Boat to China

By Frank Loesser

Out on the bri - ny _____ with a moon big and

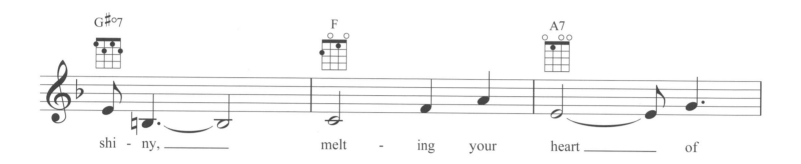

shi - ny, _____ melt - ing your heart _____ of

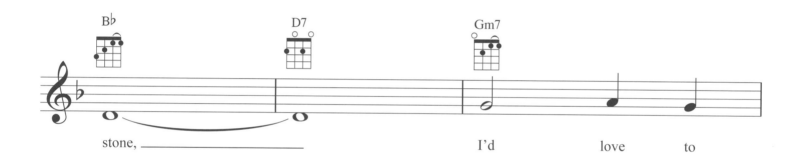

stone, _____ I'd love to

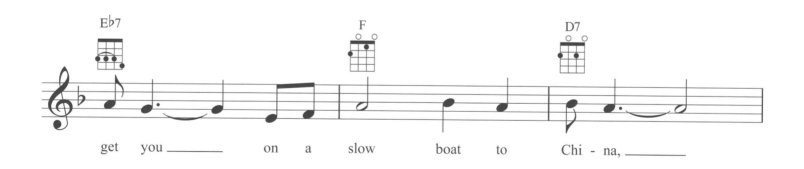

get you _____ on a slow boat to Chi - na, _____

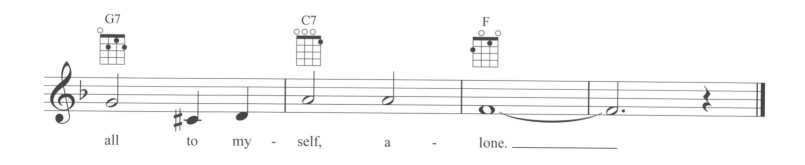

all to my - self, a - lone. _____

On the Street Where You Live

from MY FAIR LADY
Words by Alan Jay Lerner
Music by Frederick Loewe

First note

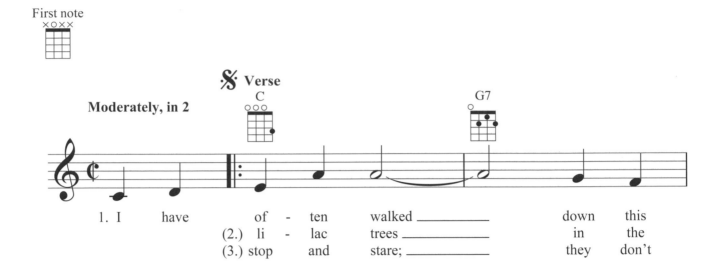

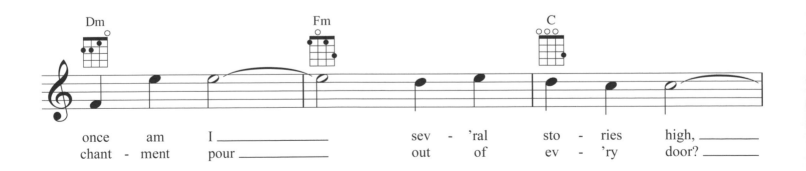

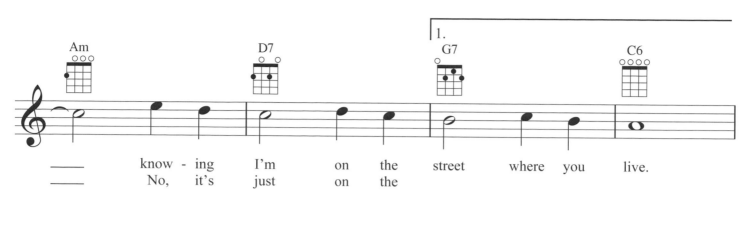

know - ing I'm on the street where you live.
No, it's just on the

2. Are there street where you live. _____ And,

Bridge

oh, _____ the tow - er - ing feel - ing, _____

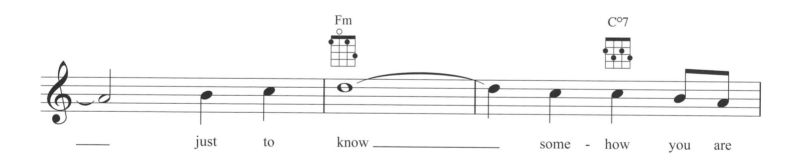

_____ just to know _____ some - how you are

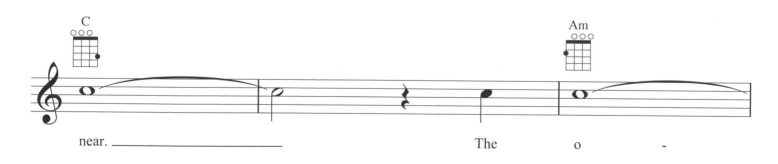

near. _____ The o -

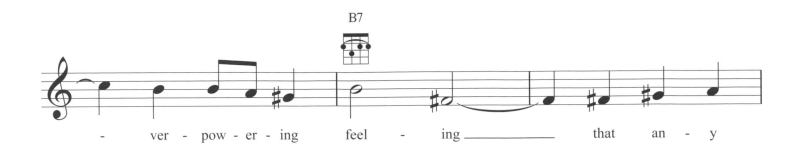

-ver - pow - er - ing feel - ing _____ that an - y

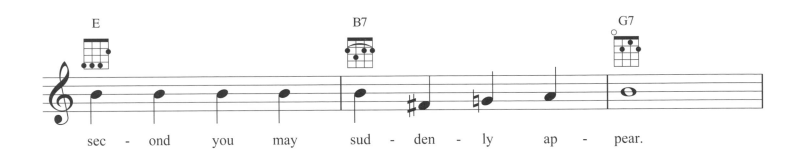

sec - ond you may sud - den - ly ap - pear.

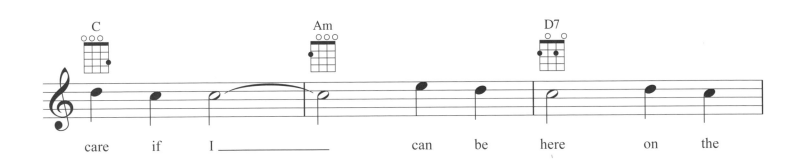

D.S. al Coda

3. Peo - ple

Coda

time go by; _____ I won't

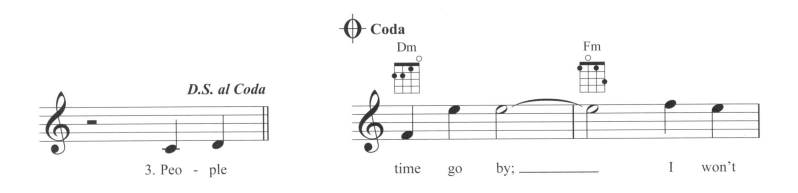

care if I _____ can be here on the

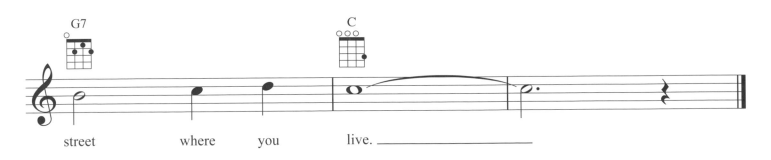

street where you live. _____

Stardust

Words by Mitchell Parish
Music by Hoagy Carmichael

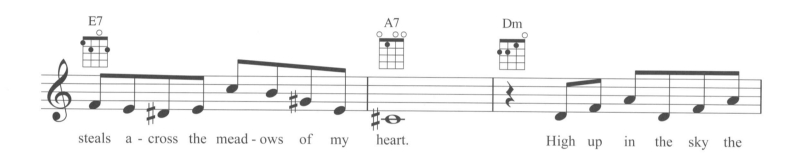

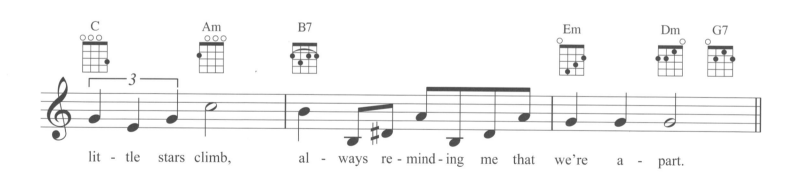

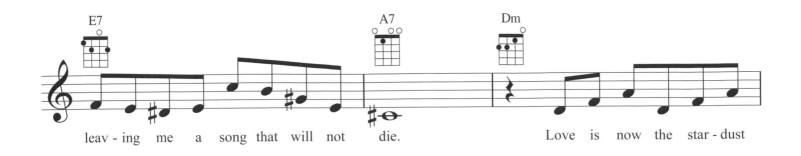

leav - ing me a song that will not die. Love is now the star - dust

of yes - ter - day, the mu - sic of the years gone by. _____ Some - times I

𝄋 Chorus

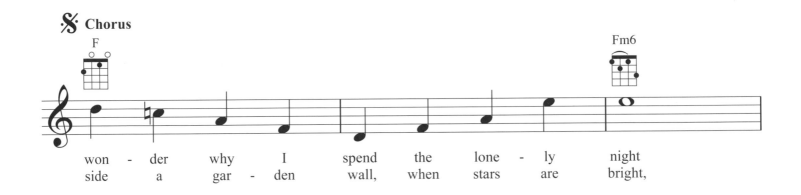

won - der why I spend the lone - ly night
side a gar - den wall, when stars are bright,

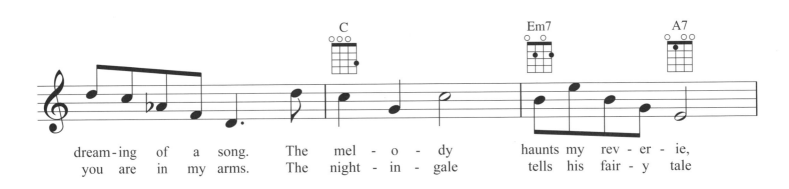

dream - ing of a song. The mel - o - dy haunts my rev - er - ie,
you are in my arms. The night - in - gale tells his fair - y tale

To Coda ⊕

and I am once a - gain with you, _____ when our love was new,
of par - a - dise, where ros - es grew. _____ Though I

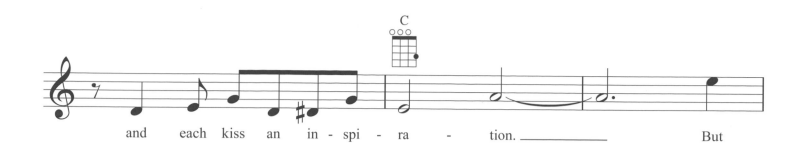

and each kiss an in - spi - ra - tion. _____ But

that was long a - go; now my con - so - la - tion is in the star - dust of a

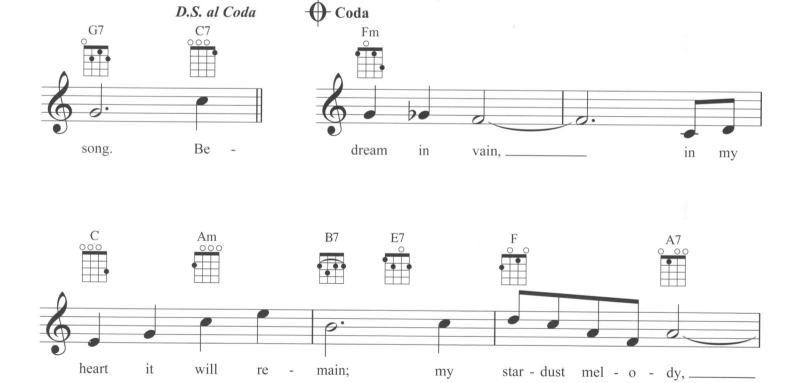

D.S. al Coda Coda

song. Be -

dream in vain, _____ in my

heart it will re - main; my star - dust mel - o - dy, _____

_____ the mem - o - ry of love's re - frain. _____

On the Sunny Side of the Street

Lyric by Dorothy Fields
Music by Jimmy McHugh

Out of Nowhere

from the Paramount Picture DUDE RANCH
Words by Edward Heyman
Music by Johnny Green

You came to me _____ from out of no - where. _____

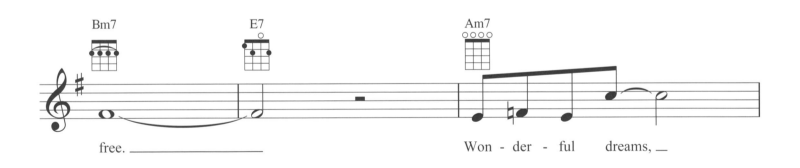

_____ You took my heart _____ and found it

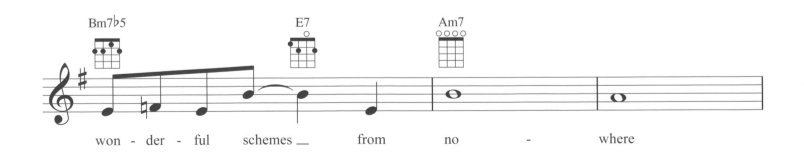

free. _____ Won - der - ful dreams, _____

won - der - ful schemes _____ from no - where

made ev - 'ry hour   sweet as a flow - er for   me. _____

If you should go _____ back to your no - where, _____

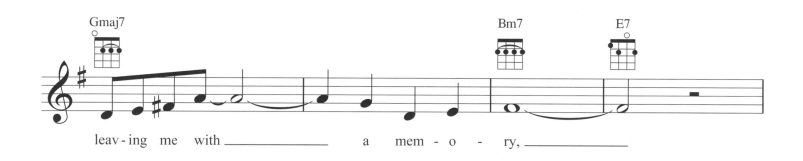

leav - ing me with _____ a mem - o - ry, _____

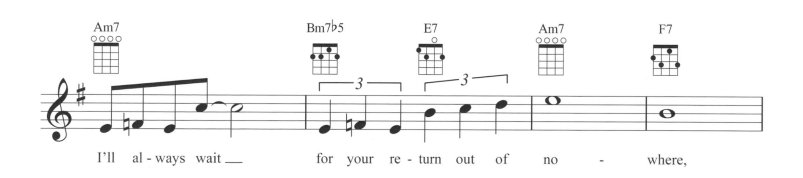

I'll al - ways wait ___   for your re - turn out of no - where,

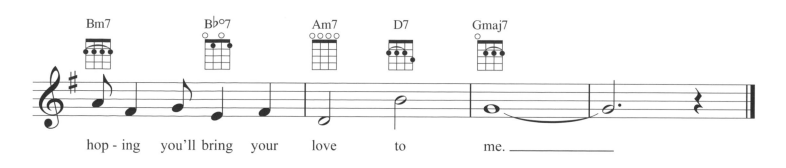

hop - ing you'll bring your love to   me. _____

People Will Say We're in Love

from OKLAHOMA!
Lyrics by Oscar Hammerstein II
Music by Richard Rodgers

1. Don't throw bou-quets at me.
3. Don't praise my charm too much.

Don't please my folks too much.
Don't look so vain with me.

Don't laugh at my jokes too much.
Don't stand in the rain with me.

Peo - ple will say we're in love!
Peo - ple will say we're in love!

2. Don't sigh and gaze at me.
4. Don't take my arm too much.

Polka Dots and Moonbeams

Words by Johnny Burke
Music by Jimmy Van Heusen

Bridge

spar-kled on a pug-nosed dream. __ There were ques-tions in the

eyes of oth-er danc-ers as we float-ed o-ver the floor. There were

ques-tions, but my heart knew all the an-swers, and per-haps a

Outro-Verse

few things more. __ Now in a cot-tage built of li-lacs and laugh-ter,

I know the mean-ing of the words "ev-er af-ter." And I'll al-ways see

pol-ka dots and moon-beams when I kiss the pug-nosed dream. __

Que Sera, Sera

(Whatever Will Be, Will Be)

from THE MAN WHO KNEW TOO MUCH
Words and Music by Jay Livingston and Raymond B. Evans

ours   to   see.   Que se - ra,   se - ra! _____

_____   What will   be   will   be!" _____

N.C.   3.   Outro

_____   2. When I grew   be. _____   Que se -
3. Now I have

ra,   se - ra! _____

Additional Lyrics

2. When I grew up and fell in love,
    I asked my sweetheart, "What lies ahead?
    Will we have rainbows day after day?"
    Here's what my sweetheart said:

3. Now I have children of my own;
    They ask their mother, "What will I be?
    Will I be pretty? Will I be rich?"
    I tell them tenderly:

Satin Doll

Words by Johnny Mercer, Billy Strayhorn and Duke Ellington
Music by Duke Ellington

Bridge

Gm7   C7   Gm7   C7

no - bod - y's fool, ___ so I'm play - ing it cool ___ as can be. ___

Fmaj7   F6   Am7   D7

___ I'll give it a whirl, __ but I ain't __

Am7   D7   Dm7   G7

___ for no girl ___ catch - ing me. _____ (Switch - a - roo - ney.)

Outro

Dm7   G7   Dm7   G7

Tel - e - phone num - bers;   well,   you   know,

Em7   A7   Em7   A7   Am7   D7

do - ing my rhum - bas   with   u - no.   And   that 'n'

A♭m7   D♭7   Cmaj7

my sat - in doll. _____

185

Skylark

Words by Johnny Mercer
Music by Hoagy Carmichael

have - n't you heard the mu - sic in the night? _____

_____ Won - der - ful mu - sic, faint as a "will - o' - the - wisp,"

cra - zy as a loon, sad as a gyp - sy ser - e -

Outro-Verse

nad - ing the moon. ___ Oh, sky - lark, _____ I don't know if I can

find these things, _____ but my heart is rid - ing on your wings. _____

_____ So, if you see them an - y - where, won't you lead me there?

Somebody Loves Me

from GEORGE WHITE'S SCANDALS OF 1924
Music by George Gershwin
Lyrics by B.G. DeSylva and Ballard MacDonald
French Version by Emelia Renaud

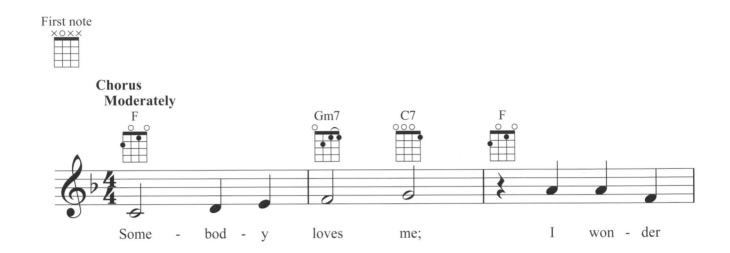

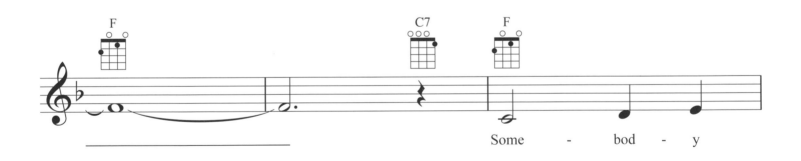

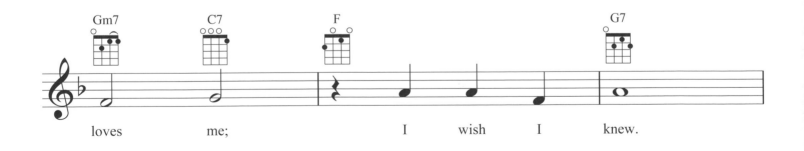

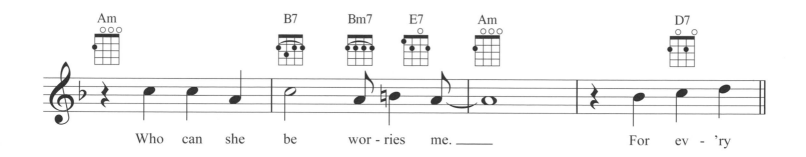

Who can she be wor - ries me. _____ For ev - 'ry

Bridge

girl who pass - es me, I shout, "Hey! May - be

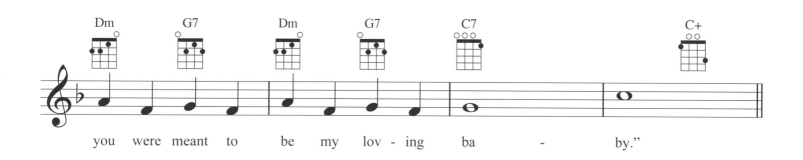

you were meant to be my lov - ing ba - by."

Outro-Chorus

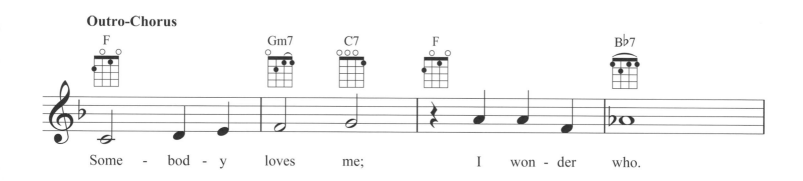

Some - bod - y loves me; I won - der who.

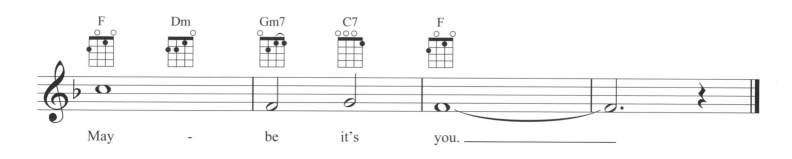

May - be it's you. _____

Stella by Starlight

from the Paramount Picture THE UNINVITED
Words by Ned Washington
Music by Victor Young

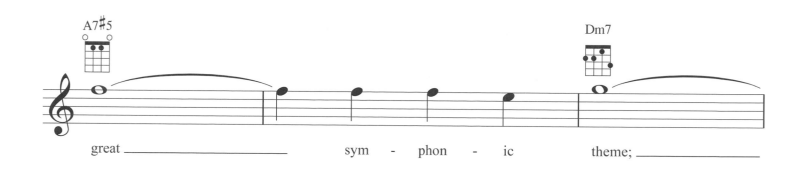

great _____ sym - phon - ic theme; _____

_____ that's Stel - la by star - light, _____ and not a

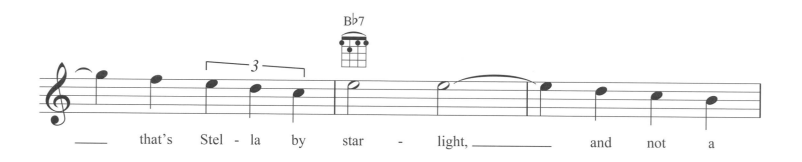

dream. _____

Boy: My heart _____
Girl: He's all _____

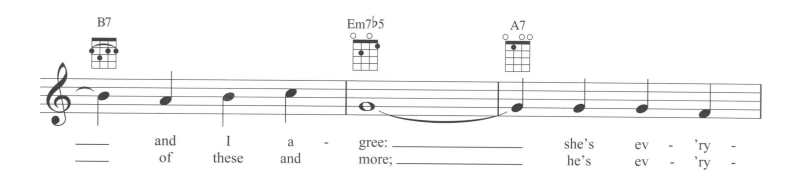

_____ and I a - gree: _____ she's ev - 'ry -
_____ of these and more; _____ he's ev - 'ry -

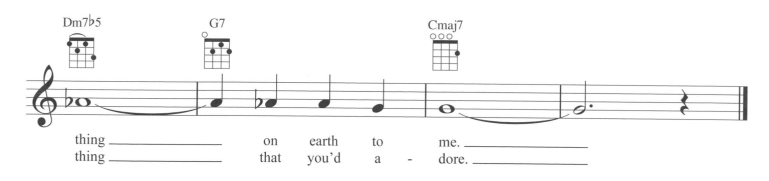

thing _____ on earth to me. _____
thing _____ that you'd a - dore. _____

191

Stormy Weather

(Keeps Rainin' All the Time)

from COTTON CLUB PARADE OF 1933
Words by Ted Koehler
Music by Harold Arlen

1. Don't know why there's no sun up in the sky, storm-y
(2.) bare, gloom and mis-'ry ev-'ry-where, storm-y

weath-er. _____ Since my man and I ain't to-geth-er, _____
weath-er. _____ Just can't get my poor self to-geth-er. _____

1.
keeps rain-in' all the time. _____ 2. Life is
So wea-ry all the

2.
time, _____ the time, _____ so wea-ry all the

The Surrey with the Fringe on Top

from OKLAHOMA!
Lyrics by Oscar Hammerstein II
Music by Richard Rodgers

Swanee

Words by Irving Caesar
Music by George Gershwin

Take the "A" Train

Words and Music by Billy Strayhorn

Thanks for the Memory

from the Paramount Picture BIG BROADCAST OF 1938
Words and Music by Leo Robin and Ralph Rainger

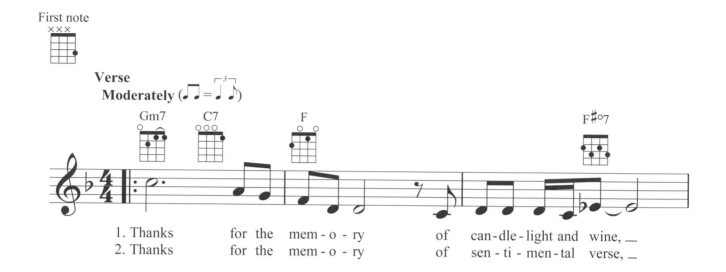

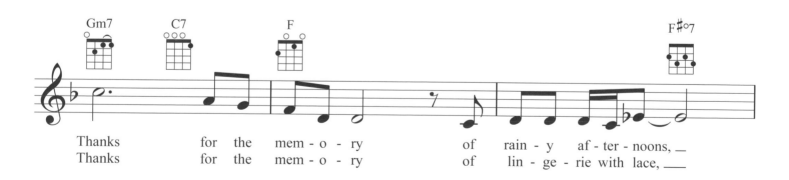

swing - y Har - lem tunes, __ and mo - tor trips and burn - ing lips and
Pils - ner by the case, __ and how I jumped the day you trumped my

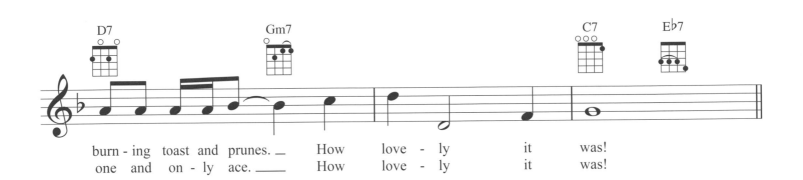

burn - ing toast and prunes. _ How love - ly it was!
one and on - ly ace. ___ How love - ly it was!

Bridge

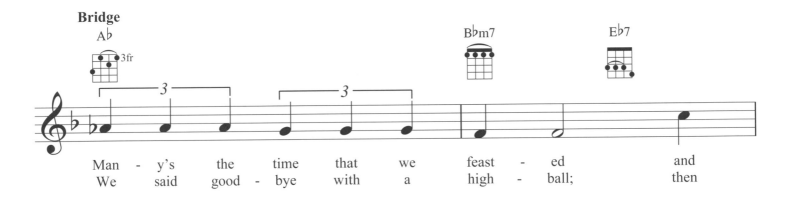

Man - y's the time that we feast - ed and
We said good - bye with a high - ball; then

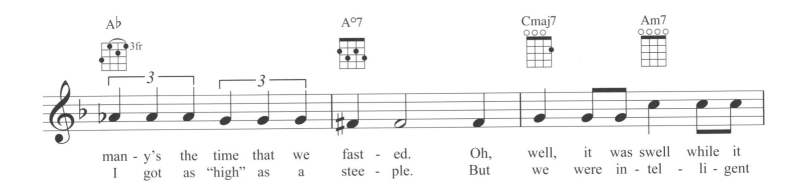

man - y's the time that we fast - ed. Oh, well, it was swell while it
I got as "high" as a stee - ple. But we were in - tel - li - gent

last - ed; we did have fun and no harm done. And
peo - ple; no tears, no fuss, hur - ray for us. So

Outro-Verse

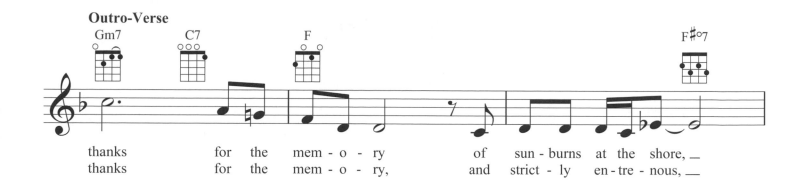

thanks   for the mem - o - ry   of sun - burns at the shore, __
thanks   for the mem - o - ry,   and strict - ly en - tre - nous, __

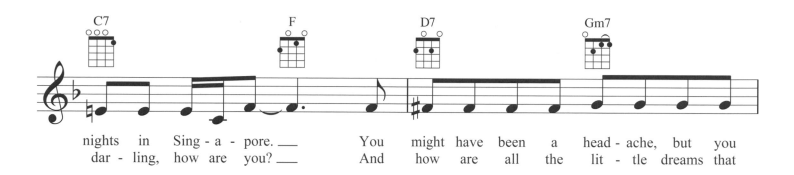

nights in Sing - a - pore. __   You might have been a head - ache, but you
dar - ling, how are you? __   And how are all the lit - tle dreams that

1.

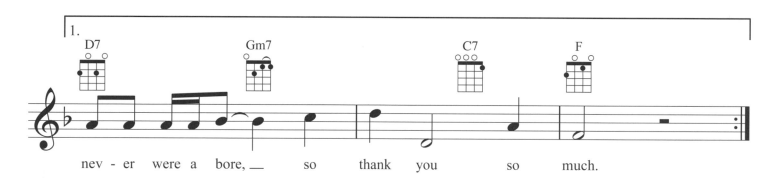

nev - er were a bore, __ so thank you so much.

2.

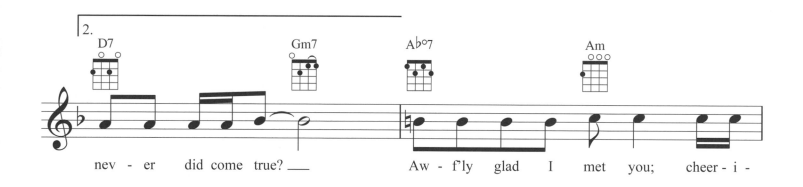

nev - er did come true? __   Aw - f'ly glad I met you; cheer - i -

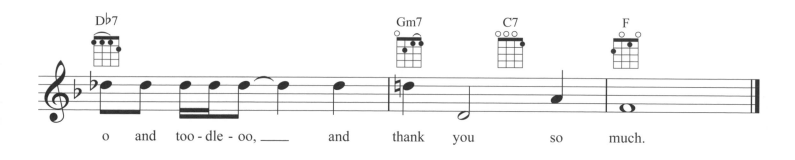

o and too - dle - oo, ___ and thank you so much.

Tangerine

from the Paramount Picture THE FLEET'S IN
Words by Johnny Mercer
Music by Victor Schertzinger

sigh. _____ And I've seen _____ toasts to Tan - ger - ine _____ raised in ev - 'ry bar a - cross the Ar - gen - tine. _____ Yes, she has them all on the run, but her heart be - longs to just one. Her heart be - longs to Tan - ger - ine. _____

Teach Me Tonight

Words by Sammy Cahn
Music by Gene De Paul

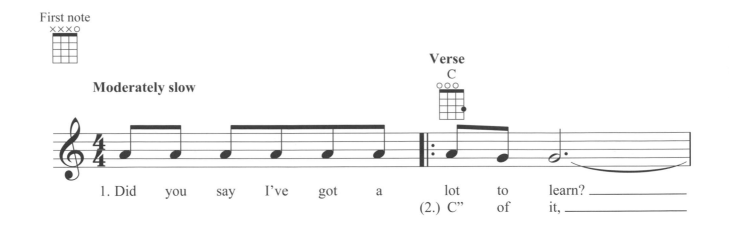

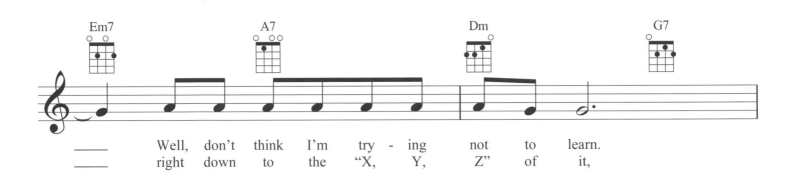

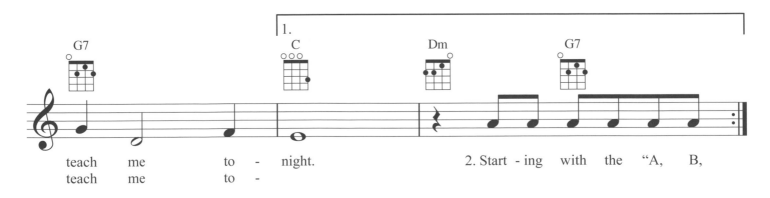

night.   The   sky's   a   black - board   high   a -

bove   you.   If   a   shoot - ing   star   goes   by, _____   I'll   use   that

star   to   write   "I   love   you"   a   thou - sand   times   a - cross   the

Outro-Verse

sky.   One   thing   is - n't   ver - y   clear,   my   love. _____   Should   the   teach - er   stand   so

near,   my   love? _____   Grad - u - a - tion's   al - most

here,   my   love.   Teach   me   to - night. _____

That Old Feeling

Words and Music by Lew Brown and Sammy Fain

First note

Chorus
Slowly, in 2

I saw you last night ___ and got that old

feel - ing. When you came in sight ___ I got that

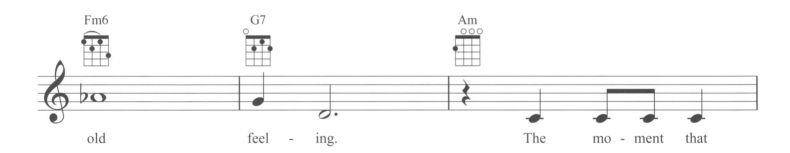

old feel - ing. The mo - ment that

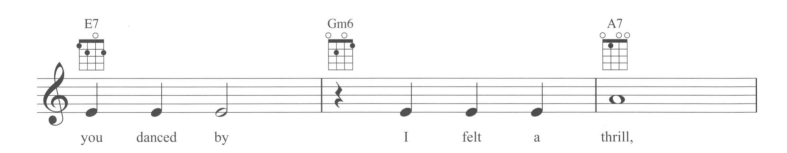

you danced by I felt a thrill,

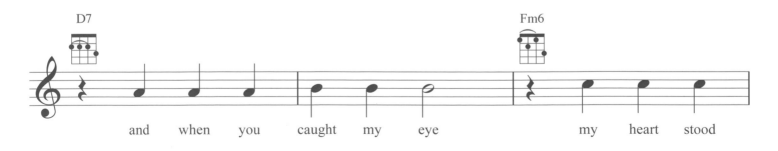

and when you caught my eye my heart stood

still. Once a - gain I seemed __ to feel that old yearn - ing, and I knew the spark __ __ of love was still burn - ing.

There'll be no new ro - mance __ for me; it's fool - ish to start, for that old feel - ing is still in my heart.

There Will Never Be Another You

from the Motion Picture ICELAND
Lyric by Mack Gordon
Music by Harry Warren

Time After Time

from the Metro-Goldwyn-Mayer Picture IT HAPPENED IN BROOKLYN
Words by Sammy Cahn
Music by Jule Styne

First note

Chorus
Moderately, in 2

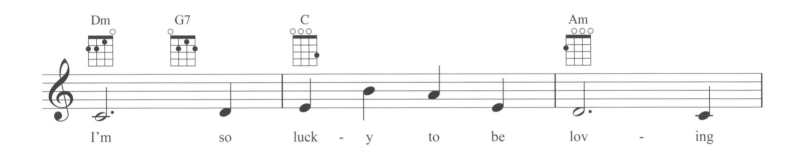

Time af - ter time I tell my - self that

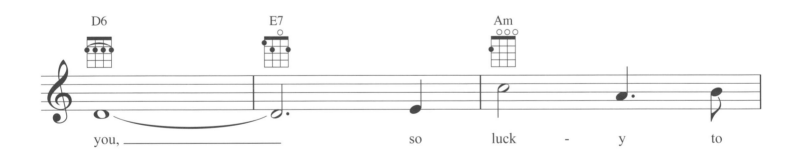

I'm so luck - y to be lov - ing

you, _____ so luck - y to

be the one you run to see in the

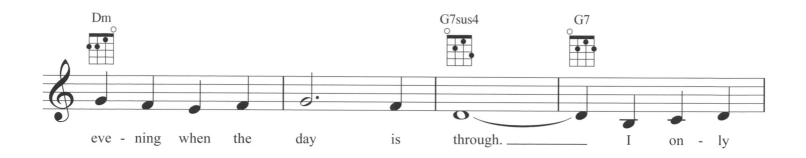

eve - ning when the day is through. _____ I on - ly

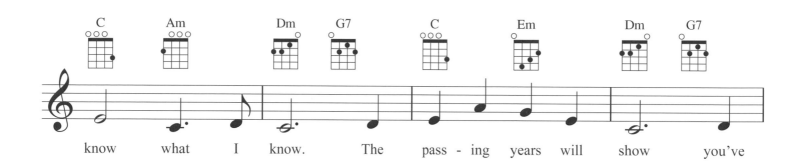

know what I know. The pass - ing years will show you've

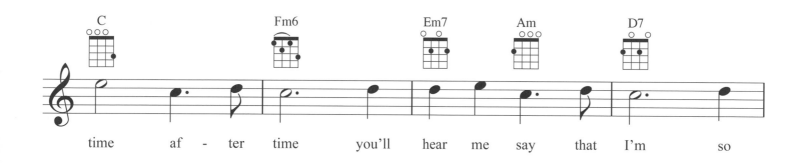

kept my love so young, so new. _____ And

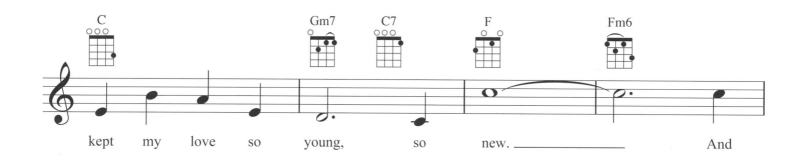

time af - ter time you'll hear me say that I'm so

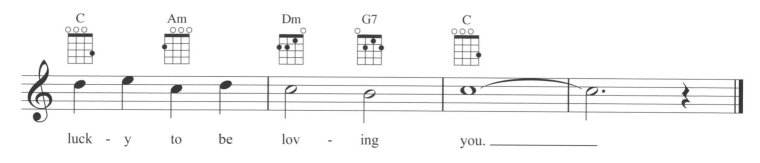

luck - y to be lov - ing you. _____

Too Late Now

from ROYAL WEDDING
Words by Alan Jay Lerner
Music by Burton Lane

First note

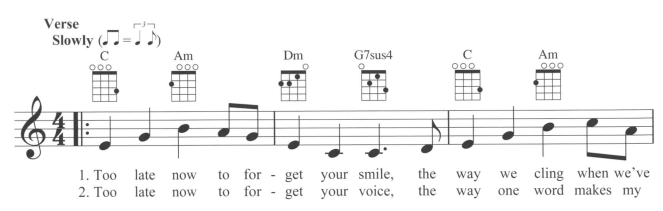

1. Too late now to for-get your smile, the way we cling when we've
2. Too late now to for-get your voice, the way one word makes my

danced a-while. Too late now to for-get and go on to
heart re-joice. Too late now to i-mag-ine my-self a-

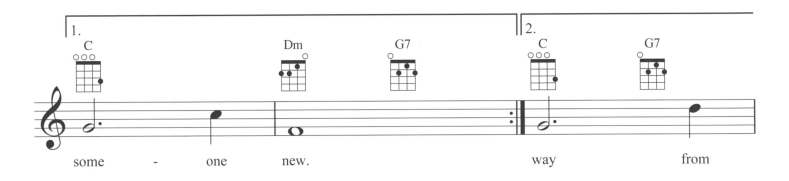

1.
some - one new.

way   from

2.
Bridge

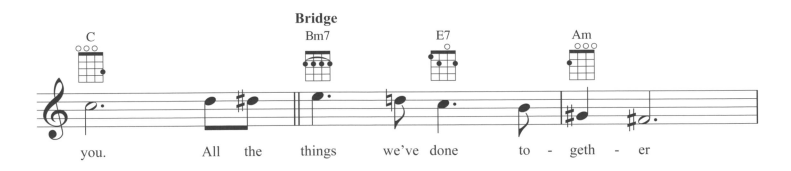

you.   All the things we've done to-geth-er

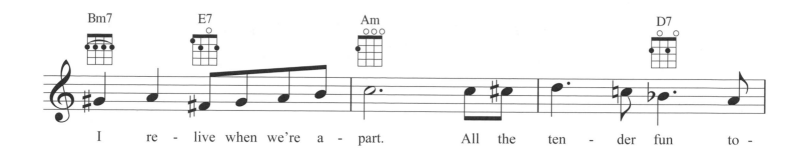

I re - live when we're a - part. All the ten - der fun to -

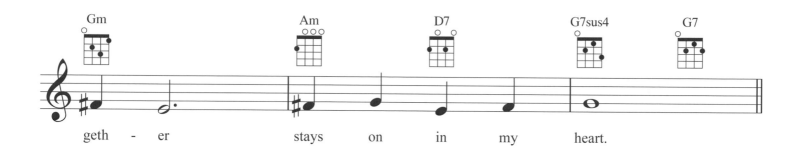

geth - er stays on in my heart.

Outro-Verse

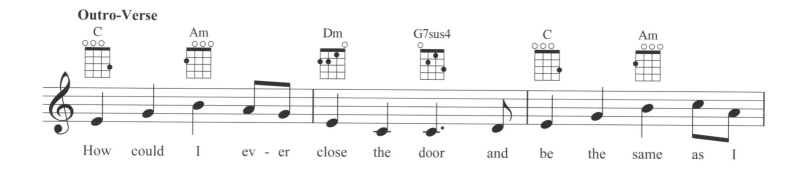

How could I ev - er close the door and be the same as I

was be - fore? Dar - ling, no, no, I can't an - y - more; it's

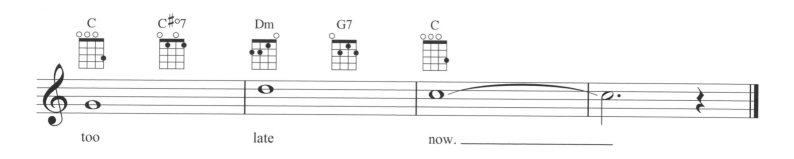

too late now. _____

Two Sleepy People

from the Paramount Motion Picture THANKS FOR THE MEMORY
Words by Frank Loesser
Music by Hoagy Carmichael

When I Fall in Love

from ONE MINUTE TO ZERO
Words by Edward Heyman
Music by Victor Young

Chorus

sun. When I give my heart, it will be com -

plete - ly, or I'll nev - er give my heart. _____

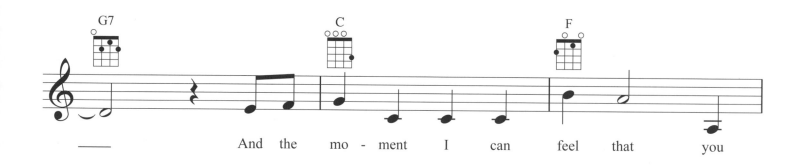

_____ And the mo - ment I can feel that you

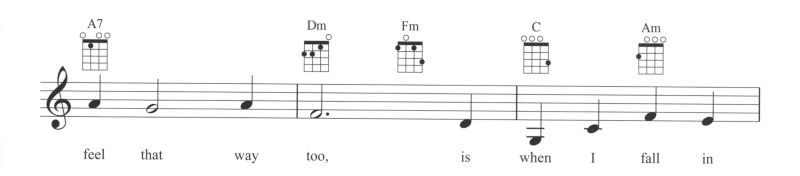

feel that way too, is when I fall in

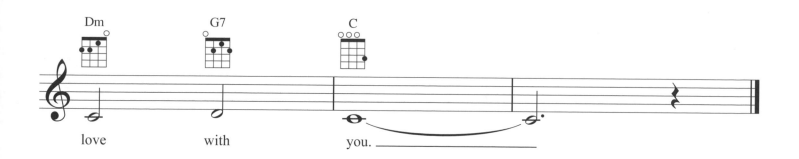

love with you. _____

When You Wish Upon a Star

from PINOCCHIO
Words by Ned Washington
Music by Leigh Harline

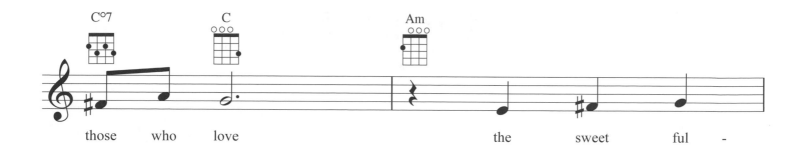

those who love ... the sweet ful -

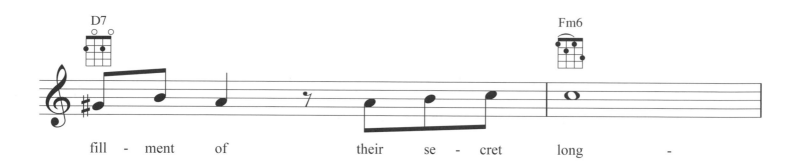

fill - ment of ... their se - cret long -

Chorus

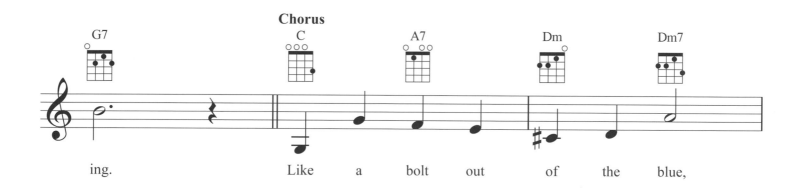

ing. ... Like a bolt out of the blue,

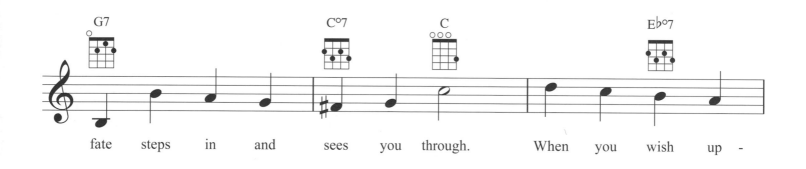

fate steps in and sees you through. When you wish up -

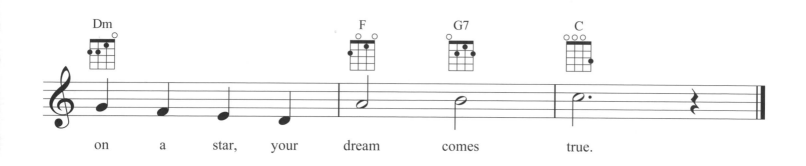

on a star, your dream comes true.

Witchcraft

Music by Cy Coleman
Lyrics by Carolyn Leigh

witch - craft, ___ and ___ al - though I ___ know ___ it's strict - ly ta -

boo, ___ when you a - rouse the need ___ in me,

my heart says, "Yes, in - deed," ___ in me. "Pro - ceed with

Outro-Verse

what you're lead - in' me to!" ___ It's such an

an - cient pitch, ___ but one I would - n't switch, ___

'cause there's no nic - er witch ___ than you! ___

Yes Sir, That's My Baby

Lyrics by Gus Kahn
Music by Walter Donaldson

You'd Be So Nice to Come Home To

from SOMETHING TO SHOUT ABOUT
Words and Music by Cole Porter

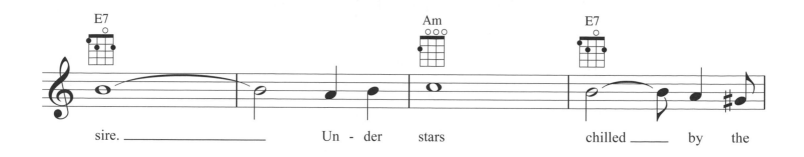

sire. _____ Un - der stars chilled _____ by the

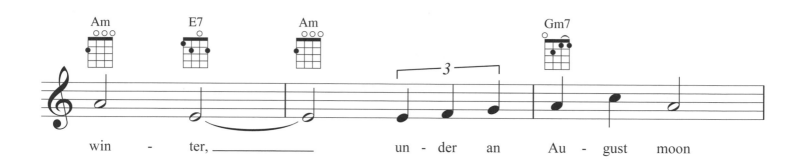

win - ter, _____ un - der an Au - gust moon

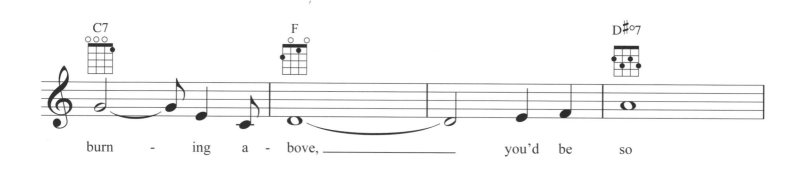

burn - ing a - bove, _____ you'd be so

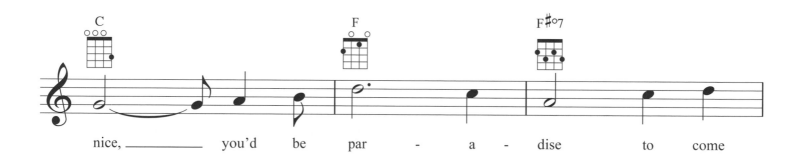

nice, _____ you'd be par - a - dise to come

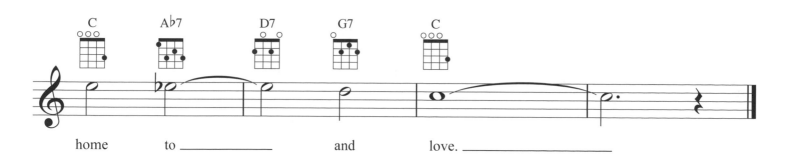

home to _____ and love. _____

That Old Black Magic

from the Paramount Picture STAR SPANGLED RHYTHM
Words by Johnny Mercer
Music by Harold Arlen

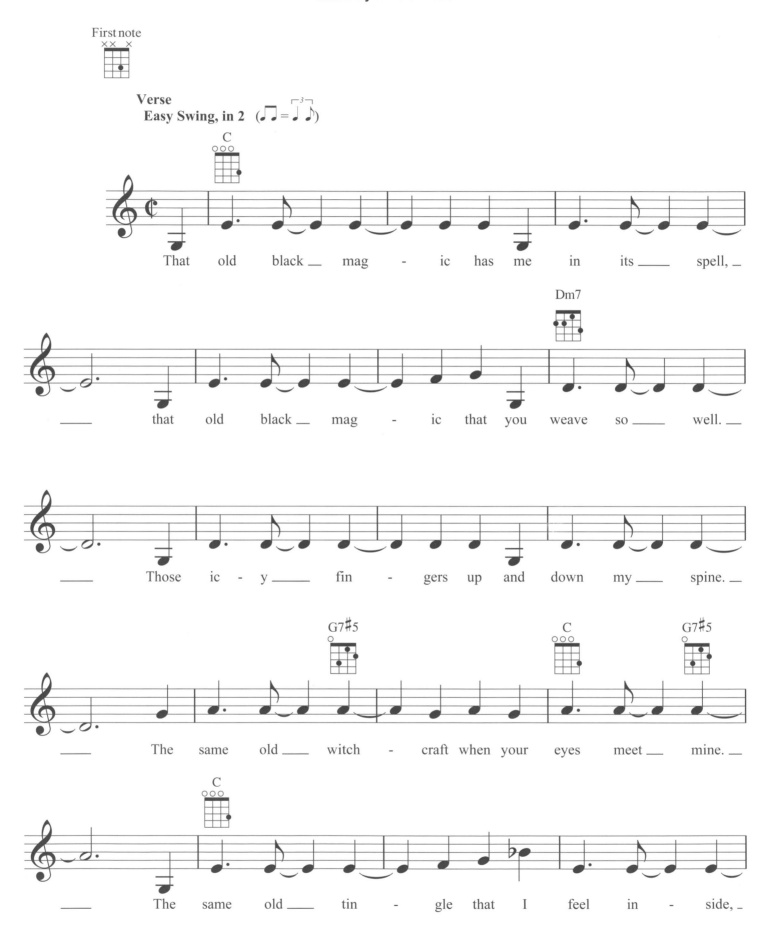

and then that el - e - va - tor starts its ride, and

down and down I go, 'round and 'round I go,

like a leaf that's caught in the tide. I should

Bridge

stay a - way, but what can I do? I hear your name

and I'm a - flame, a - flame with such a burn-ing de-

sire that on - ly your kiss can put out the

Outro Verse

fire. _____ For you're the _____ lov - er I have wait - ed _____ for, _____

_____ the mate that _____ fate _____ had me cre - at - ed _____ for. _____

_____ And ev - 'ry _____ time _____ your lips meet mine, _____

_____ dar - ling, down and _____ down _____ I go, 'round and _____ 'round _____

_____ I go in a _____ spin, _____ lov - ing the spin I'm _____ in, _____

_____ un - der that old black _____ mag - ic called love! _____

Hal•Leonard® UKULELE PLAY-ALONG

AUDIO ACCESS INCLUDED

Now you can play your favorite songs on your uke with great-sounding backing tracks to help you sound like a bona fide pro! The audio also features playback tools so you can adjust the tempo without changing the pitch and loop challenging parts.

1. POP HITS
00701451 Book/CD Pack................$15.99

2. UKE CLASSICS
00701452 Book/CD Pack................$15.99

3. HAWAIIAN FAVORITES
00701453 Book/Online Audio..........$14.99

4. CHILDREN'S SONGS
00701454 Book/CD Pack................$14.99

5. CHRISTMAS SONGS
00701696 Book/CD Pack................$12.99

6. LENNON & MCCARTNEY
00701723 Book/Online Audio..........$12.99

7. DISNEY FAVORITES
00701724 Book/Online Audio..........$12.99

8. CHART HITS
00701745 Book/CD Pack................$15.99

9. THE SOUND OF MUSIC
00701784 Book/CD Pack................$14.99

10. MOTOWN
00701964 Book/CD Pack................$12.99

11. CHRISTMAS STRUMMING
00702458 Book/Online Audio..........$12.99

12. BLUEGRASS FAVORITES
00702584 Book/CD Pack................$12.99

13. UKULELE SONGS
00702599 Book/CD Pack................$12.99

14. JOHNNY CASH
00702615 Book/CD Pack................$15.99

15. COUNTRY CLASSICS
00702834 Book/CD Pack................$12.99

16. STANDARDS
00702835 Book/CD Pack................$12.99

17. POP STANDARDS
00702836 Book/CD Pack................$12.99

18. IRISH SONGS
00703086 Book/Online Audio..........$12.99

19. BLUES STANDARDS
00703087 Book/CD Pack................$12.99

20. FOLK POP ROCK
00703088 Book/CD Pack................$12.99

21. HAWAIIAN CLASSICS
00703097 Book/CD Pack................$12.99

22. ISLAND SONGS
00703098 Book/CD Pack................$12.99

23. TAYLOR SWIFT – 2ND EDITION
00221966 Book/Online Audio..........$16.99

24. WINTER WONDERLAND
00101871 Book/CD Pack................$12.99

25. GREEN DAY
00110398 Book/CD Pack................$14.99

26. BOB MARLEY
00110399 Book/Online Audio..........$14.99

27. TIN PAN ALLEY
00116358 Book/CD Pack................$12.99

28. STEVIE WONDER
00116736 Book/CD Pack................$14.99

29. OVER THE RAINBOW & OTHER FAVORITES
00117076 Book/Online Audio..........$14.99

30. ACOUSTIC SONGS
00122336 Book/CD Pack................$14.99

31. JASON MRAZ
00124166 Book/CD Pack................$14.99

32. TOP DOWNLOADS
00127507 Book/CD Pack................$14.99

33. CLASSICAL THEMES
00127892 Book/Online Audio..........$14.99

34. CHRISTMAS HITS
00128602 Book/CD Pack................$14.99

35. SONGS FOR BEGINNERS
00129009 Book/Online Audio..........$14.99

36. ELVIS PRESLEY HAWAII
00138199 Book/Online Audio..........$14.99

37. LATIN
00141191 Book/Online Audio..........$14.99

38. JAZZ
00141192 Book/Online Audio..........$14.99

39. GYPSY JAZZ
00146559 Book/Online Audio..........$14.99

40. TODAY'S HITS
00160845 Book/Online Audio..........$14.99

Prices, contents, and availability subject to change without notice.

www.halleonard.com

Ride the Ukulele Wave!

The Beach Boys for Ukulele

This folio features 20 favorites, including: Barbara Ann • Be True to Your School • California Girls • Fun, Fun, Fun • God Only Knows • Good Vibrations • Help Me Rhonda • I Get Around • In My Room • Kokomo • Little Deuce Coupe • Sloop John B • Surfin' U.S.A. • Wouldn't It Be Nice • and more!

00701726 . . . . $14.99

Disney Songs for Ukulele

20 great Disney classics arranged for all uke players, including: Beauty and the Beast • Bibbidi-Bobbidi-Boo (The Magic Song) • Can You Feel the Love Tonight • Chim Chim Cher-ee • Heigh-Ho • It's a Small World • Some Day My Prince Will Come • We're All in This Together • When You Wish upon a Star • and more.

00701708 . . . . $14.99

Jack Johnson – Strum & Sing

Cherry Lane Music
Strum along with 41 Jack Johnson songs using this top-notch collection of chords and lyrics just for the uke! Includes: Better Together • Bubble Toes • Cocoon • Do You Remember • Flake • Fortunate Fool • Good People • Holes to Heaven • Taylor • Tomorrow Morning • and more.

02501702 . . . . $19.99

The Beatles for Ukulele

Ukulele players can strum, sing and pick along with 20 Beatles classics! Includes: All You Need Is Love • Eight Days a Week • Good Day Sunshine • Here, There and Everywhere • Let It Be • Love Me Do • Penny Lane • Yesterday • and more.

00700154 . . . . $16.99

First 50 Songs You Should Play on Ukulele

An amazing collection of 50 accessible, must-know favorites: Edelweiss • Hey, Soul Sister • I Walk the Line • I'm Yours • Imagine • Over the Rainbow • Peaceful Easy Feeling • The Rainbow Connection • Riptide • and many more.

00149250 . . . . $14.99

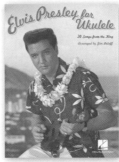

Elvis Presley for Ukulele

arr. Jim Beloff
20 classic hits from The King: All Shook Up • Blue Hawaii • Blue Suede Shoes • Can't Help Falling in Love • Don't • Heartbreak Hotel • Hound Dog • Jailhouse Rock • Love Me • Love Me Tender • Return to Sender • Suspicious Minds • Teddy Bear • and more.

00701004 . . . . $15.99

The Daily Ukulele

compiled and arranged by
Liz and Jim Beloff
Strum a different song everyday with easy arrangements of 365 of your favorite songs in one big songbook! Includes favorites by the Beatles, Beach Boys, and Bob Dylan, folk songs, pop songs, kids' songs, Christmas carols, and Broadway and Hollywood tunes, all with a spiral binding for ease of use.

00240356 . . . . $39.99

Folk Songs for Ukulele

A great collection to take along to the campfire! 60 folk songs, including: Amazing Grace • Buffalo Gals • Camptown Races • For He's a Jolly Good Fellow • Good Night Ladies • Home on the Range • I've Been Working on the Railroad • Kumbaya • My Bonnie Lies over the Ocean • On Top of Old Smoky • Scarborough Fair • Swing Low, Sweet Chariot • Take Me Out to the Ball Game • Yankee Doodle • and more.

00696068 . . . . $12.99

Jake Shimabukuro – Peace Love Ukulele

Deemed "the Hendrix of the ukulele," Hawaii native Jake Shimabukuro is a uke virtuoso. Our songbook features note-for-note transcriptions with ukulele tablature of Jake's masterful playing on all the CD tracks: Bohemian Rhapsody • Boy Meets Girl • Bring Your Adz • Hallelujah • Pianoforte 2010 • Variation on a Dance 2010 • and more, plus two bonus selections!

00702516 . . . . $19.99

The Daily Ukulele – Leap Year Edition

366 More Songs for Better Living
compiled and arranged by
Liz and Jim Beloff
An amazing second volume with 366 MORE songs for you to master each day of a leap year! Includes: Ain't No Sunshine • Calendar Girl • I Got You Babe • Lean on Me • Moondance • and many, many more.

00240681 . . . . $39.99

Hawaiian Songs for Ukulele

Over thirty songs from the state that made the ukulele famous, including: Beyond the Rainbow • Hanalei Moon • Ka-lu-a • Lovely Hula Girl • Mele Kalikimaka • One More Aloha • Sea Breeze • Tiny Bubbles • Waikiki • and more.

00696065 . . . . $10.99

Worship Songs for Ukulele

25 worship songs: Amazing Grace (My Chains are Gone) • Blessed Be Your Name • Enough • God of Wonders • Holy Is the Lord • How Great Is Our God • In Christ Alone • Love the Lord • Mighty to Save • Sing to the King • Step by Step • We Fall Down • and more.

00702546 . . . . $14.99

HAL•LEONARD®

UKULELE ENSEMBLE SERIES

The songs in these collections are playable by any combination of ukuleles (soprano, concert, tenor or baritone). Each arrangement features the melody, a harmony part, and a "bass" line. Chord symbols are also provided if you wish to add a rhythm part. For groups with more than three or four ukuleles, the parts may be doubled.

CHRISTMAS CAROLS
Early Intermediate Level

Away in a Manger • Carol of the Bells • Deck the Hall • The First Noel • God Rest Ye Merry, Gentlemen • Hark! the Herald Angels Sing • It Came Upon the Midnight Clear • Jingle Bells • Joy to the World • O Christmas Tree • O Come, All Ye Faithful • O Holy Night • O Little Town of Bethlehem • Silent Night • Up on the Housetop.
00129248 .... $9.99

CHRISTMAS SONGS
Early Intermediate Level

The Chipmunk Song • The Christmas Song (Chestnuts Roasting on an Open Fire) • Do You Hear What I Hear • Feliz Navidad • Frosty the Snow Man • Have Yourself a Merry Little Christmas • Here Comes Santa Claus (Right Down Santa Claus Lane) • A Holly Jolly Christmas • (There's No Place Like) Home for the Holidays • Jingle Bell Rock • The Little Drummer Boy • Merry Christmas, Darling • The Most Wonderful Time of the Year • Silver Bells • White Christmas.
00129247 .... $9.99

CLASSIC ROCK
Mid-Intermediate Level

Aqualung • Behind Blue Eyes • Born to Be Wild • Crazy Train • Fly Like an Eagle • Free Bird • Hey Jude • Low Rider • Moondance • Oye Como Va • Proud Mary • (I Can't Get No) Satisfaction • Smoke on the Water • Summertime Blues • Sunshine of Your Love.
00103904 .... $9.99

DISNEY FAVORITES
Early Intermediate Level

The Bare Necessities • Beauty and the Beast • Can You Feel the Love Tonight • Colors of the Wind • A Dream Is a Wish Your Heart Makes • It's a Small World • Let It Go • Let's Go Fly a Kite • Little April Shower • Mickey Mouse March • Seize the Day • The Siamese Cat Song • Supercalifragilisticexpialidocious • Under the Sea • A Whole New World.
00279513 .... $9.99

HAWAIIAN SONGS
Mid-Intermediate Level

Aloha Oe • Beyond the Rainbow • Harbor Lights • Hawaiian War Chant (Ta-Hu-Wa-Hu-Wai) • The Hawaiian Wedding Song (Ke Kali Nei Au) • Ka-lu-a • Lovely Hula Hands • Mele Kalikimaka • The Moon of Manakoora • One Paddle, Two Paddle • Pearly Shells (Pupu 'O 'Ewa) • Red Sails in the Sunset • Sleepy Lagoon • Song of the Islands • Tiny Bubbles.
00119254 .... $9.99

THE NUTCRACKER
Late Intermediate Level

Arabian Dance ("Coffee") • Chinese Dance ("Tea") • Dance of the Reed-Flutes • Dance of the Sugar Plum Fairy • March • Overture • Russian Dance ("Trepak") • Waltz of the Flowers.
00119908 .... $9.99

ROCK INSTRUMENTALS
Late Intermediate Level

Beck's Bolero • Cissy Strut • Europa (Earth's Cry Heaven's Smile) • Frankenstein • Green Onions • Jessica • Misirlou • Perfidia • Pick Up the Pieces • Pipeline • Rebel 'Rouser • Sleepwalk • Tequila • Walk Don't Run • Wipe Out.
00103909 .... $9.99

STANDARDS & GEMS
Mid-Intermediate Level

Autumn Leaves • Cheek to Cheek • Easy to Love • Fly Me to the Moon • I Only Have Eyes for You • It Had to Be You • Laura • Mack the Knife • My Funny Valentine • Theme from "New York, New York" • Over the Rainbow • Satin Doll • Some Day My Prince Will Come • Summertime • The Way You Look Tonight.
00103898 .... $9.99

THEME MUSIC
Mid-Intermediate Level

Batman Theme • Theme from E.T. (The Extra-Terrestrial) • Forrest Gump – Main Title (Feather Theme) • The Godfather (Love Theme) • Hawaii Five-O Theme • He's a Pirate • Linus and Lucy • Mission: Impossible Theme • Peter Gunn • The Pink Panther • Raiders March • (Ghost) Riders in the Sky (A Cowboy Legend) • Theme from Spider Man • Theme from "Star Trek®" • Theme from "Superman."
00103903 .... $9.99

www.halleonard.com